BORIS YELTSIN
First President of Russia

Champions of Freedom

BORIS YELTSIN
First President of Russia

Calvin Craig Miller

MORGAN
REYNOLDS
Incorporated

Greensboro

BORIS YELTSIN
First President of Russia

Library of Congress Cataloging-in-Publication Data
Miller, Calvin Craig, 1954-
    Boris Yeltsin, first president of Russia / Calvin Craig Miller. — 1st ed.
        p.   cm. -- (Champions of freedom)
    Includes bibliographical references and index.
    ISBN 1-883846-08-0
        1. Yeltsin, Boris Nikolayevich, 1931- —Juvenile literature.   2. Presidents—Russia
(Federation)—Biography—Juvenile literature.   3. Politicians--Soviet Union--Biography—
Juvenile literature. 4. Soviet Union—Politics and government—1985-1991—Juvenile
literature. 5. Russia (Federation)—Politics and government—1991-Juvenile literature.
[1. Yeltsin, Boris Nikolayevich, 1931- . 2. Presidents—Russia (Federation)] I. Title
II. Series: Champions of freedom (Greensboro, NC)
DK290.3.Y45M55   1994
947.086--dc20

                                                                94-16562
                                                                CIP

Printed in the United States of America

First Edition

5 4 3 2 1

In memory of my father, Wells Arlen Miller,
this book is dedicated to my mother, Violet E. Connell and to
the Rev. Frederick F. Dancy

CONTENTS

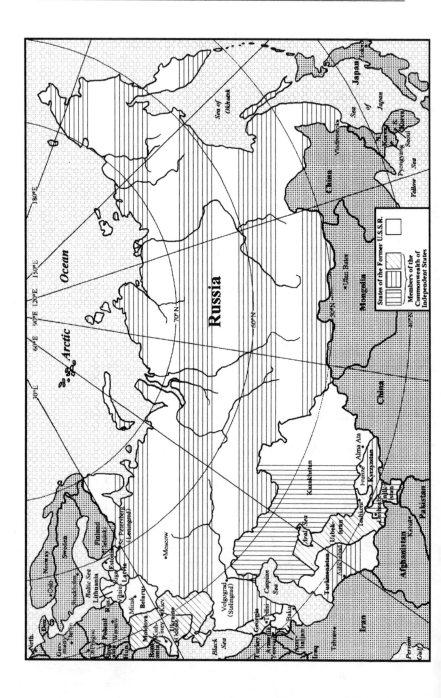

PROLOGUE

The tanks rolled into Moscow just after sunrise on October 4, 1993. While most of the city's people hurried off to work, the tanks encircled the towering white building Russians call the White House. Lined up behind the tanks were personnel carriers, filled with Commandos preparing to storm the structure.

Russian President Boris Yeltsin had given the orders to lay siege to the White House. Inside the building huddled the meager forces of two men who had once been Yeltsin's staunchest allies: Vice-President Alexander Rutskoi, and Parliament Chairman Ruslan Khasbulatov, who, two years before, had stood with Yeltsin during an attempted coup by disgruntled communist hardliners.

But now Yeltsin and the two men were enemies. In the

power struggle that followed the coup, Rutskoi and Khasbulatov had opposed Yeltsin on the question of how Russia should be run. The two men had tried to strip him of his most important powers. On September 21, Yeltsin had responded by dissolving Parliament. A crisis that threatened the future of the Russian Republic ensued.

On this sunny fall Monday the crisis would end. Yeltsin's ememies would be struck down by the Russian military.

Gunfire burst against the white walls just as the rush hour began. Puffs of smoke billowed out of the windows on the east side. The defenders shot back with rifles and threw firebombs. Army troops, ordered to take the building, raced across the lawn under a rain of bullets. The barrels of the T-72 tanks shuddered as they fired round after round into the 19-story White House.

Fires raged on the top floors; orange flames spilled from the windows. Paper fluttered into the streets, followed by billows of heavy, black smoke. As hope for a rescue began to run out inside the White House, some of the rebels prayed while others swore. After 10 hours of the siege, they surrendered. Haggard and weary, the last members of the defiant parliament marched out of the building. They appeared dazed, surprised at the violent measures Yeltsin had taken against them, and the lack of support they had received from their fellow Russians.

Who is Boris Yeltsin, and why did the series of events that had started so positively with the successful overthrow of the attempted Communist seizure of power in August, 1991, result in violence only two years later? The answers to these question are not simple, especially for anyone who takes the processes of democracy for granted. Some of the answers can be found in the national character of Russia itself, and the difficulties the country has experienced trying to replace 70 years of totalitarian control with democracy. But other answers can only be found in the makeup of Boris Yeltsin, a tough politician who seems to thrive on fights and controversies.

Evaluating Boris Yeltsin is no easy task. The best way to begin is with his early life, when his enemies were not opposing politicians; but hunger, poverty, and the long Siberian winter.

ONE

FARM BOY

Boris Yeltsin suffered his first life-threatening ordeal at the hands of a drunken priest. It happened at his christening in the Russian village of Butko, not long after his birth on February 1, 1931.

Christening is the ritual of naming and baptizing an infant. Although the communist state of the 1930s frowned on religion, many Russians still observed the ceremony. People in Boris' home village of Butko, in the province of Sverdlovsk, were mostly farmers who revered the old traditions. Yeltsin's parents, Klavdia and Nikolai, were determined their first born would be anointed in spirit. There was little else the poor family could give him.

It was traditional for parents taking their child to be baptized to bring a gift of alcohol for the clergyman. The priest might taste any number of beverages from different households throughout the day—wine, beer or vodka. On that particular afternoon, visiting parents had donated generously. By the time the infant Yeltsin's turn came, the priest was tipsy.

When it came time for the baby to be baptized, the holy man dropped him into the baptismal fountain.

As the youngest Yeltsin sank to the bottom, the inebriated priest got into an argument with one of his parishioners, and forgot about the business at hand. When she saw her baby about to drown, Klavdia Yeltsin screamed and fished him from the fountain.

The near-drowning left the priest unruffled. "Well, if he can survive such an ordeal, he's a good tough lad," the priest said. "And I name him Boris."[1] The name came from a Russian word meaning "to fight." And it has certainly proven to be an apt description.

Millions of families in the Soviet Union of the 1930s had to fight, just to survive. The country was making its way into a new system of government, Communism, under the leadership of the dictator Joseph Stalin. The Communists had smashed a 400-year line of Russian kings, or czars, during the October Revolution of 1917. Many supporters of the October Revolution held high hopes for the common

Joseph Stalin (AP/Wide World)

people in the new Union of Soviet Socialist Republics, or USSR, and Stalin at first seemed to stand among the idealists.

However, by the time of Boris Yeltsin's birth, Stalin had proven himself a murderous tyrant. He had executed and tortured his enemies, while cementing his one-man rule. The first communist leaders had founded their beliefs on the idea of the nation itself controlling all property for the good of all the country's citizens. But under his rule, the Soviet Union seemed merely to be the personal property of Joseph Stalin.

Stalin had forced millions of peasants onto collective farms, such as the one where Boris spent his childhood. These farms operated much differently from an American farm. An American farmer could have owned the land, and decided how much of each crop to plant. If he thought he could earn more by planting wheat instead of corn, he was free to do so. He could have made a decision based on economic demand. This is called capitalism, and is the basis of the most modern economies, including that of the United States.

But capitalism was a dirty word to the Communists. They considered it responsible for many evils, such as the long hours, low pay and unsafe conditions that existed in many 19th-century factories. Under Communism, the ideal was that each person would work to his or her capacity and receive in return all that they needed. The government controlled most property and sources of wealth. Government officials told the collective farms—where many families lived and worked together on government land—what to plant, and how much. The problem with this organization is obvious: what the government decides the nation should produce may not be what the people need. Under Stalin, who focused his attention on building up the industrial base of the country, the needs of the people, and especially the farmers, mattered little. Although all people were supposed to share equally in the wealth, many people shared only misery and death. Millions of people died in famines which could have been avoided in a freer economic system.

At first, Nikolai Yeltsin resisted living on a collective farm. But while the Yeltsin family did not starve, they suffered from poverty and hunger. In the early 1930s, they lived in a small house, and owned a horse and a cow. First the horse and then the cow died, leaving the family without the bare necessities of survival. Boris' father eventually was forced to move his wife and children to a collective farm.

The adjustment was not easy, as the Yeltsins moved into one of the noisy, crowded huts that housed the workers. Outlaw gangs harassed the collective farms with robbery and violence. Nikolai was only able to make ends meet by taking a laborer's job in a nearby plant producing potash, a product used in farming and industry. The family lived for ten years in a building that resembled an army barracks more than a home. During the hard Siberian winters, icy winds blew through cracks in the wall. Yeltsin's grandfather, his parents, and the three small children sometimes slept together on the floor, huddled next to their goat for warmth.

The terrible conditions of the collective farm was not the only ordeal the Yeltsins suffered during the Stalin years. Nikaloi also ran afoul of the dreaded *Cheka*, the secret police. Western societies would have considered Nikolai's "crimes" a sign of good character. Before the Communists took over, the family had owned a windmill, a threshing machine, a harvester, and some livestock. However, the secret police now listed these belongings as though they were the spoils of a burglary ring.

"Owned, owned, owned," Yeltsin wrote years later. "That was why he was guilty—he had worked a lot and had taken a lot of responsibility upon himself." [2] But that was guilt enough for a Stalinist court. Nikolai spent three years in a labor camp, as did Yeltsin's uncle. In a way, both got off lightly. Perhaps 20 million people died in such labor camps during Stalin's regime. In fact, the Yeltsin brothers may have been turned in by one of the government's paid informants, who frequently lied about innocent people to fulfill their state-set quota of people charged with crimes against the state.

As one Russian writer said of the Stalin era: "Our great goal was the universal triumph of Communism, and for the sake of that goal everything was permissible—to lie, to steal, to destroy hundreds of thousands and even millions of people." [3]

The Yeltsins considered toughness a family virtue. Yeltsin's father and grandfather shared many traits, including determination and a quick temper. Nikolai delivered stern, often cruel discipline. He was quick to beat Boris with a strap for real or imagined sins. But young Boris wanted to prove he was also tough, and turned the punishment sessions into a contest of wills as his father laid on the strap.

"I always clenched my teeth and did not make a sound, which infuriated him," Yeltsin later wrote.[4] His mother would often dash to Boris's rescue, yanking away Nikolai's strap, and throw herself between Nikolai and their stubborn son.

Boris's mother, Klavdia, was by nature as sweet-tempered and lenient as Nikoloi was demanding. While the men labored for survival, she took in sewing jobs as favors for relatives and neighbors. She never took money for her work, but would sometimes accept food for the family. Klavdia often sewed long into the night. Boris Yeltsin thought of his mother as a saint.

But Nikolai also had his good side. He considered himself an inventor, and spent many hours describing to Boris a machine which would lay bricks. He worked on the endless details, and even drew up a plan. The effort, unfortunately, ended only in frustration for Nikolai, as the device was never built.

It is hard to imagine how anyone could find joy in such a brutal upbringing. Yet Boris and his family did have good times. They shared in parties and celebrations with their

Workers meeting on a collective farm in 1939, during the Stalin era.
(Sovfoto)

neighbors. Laughter rang through the walls during birthday parties and anniversaries. The whole hut shared a record player and three or four records. Boris heard the same lyrics so many times he can still recite them today.

Unfortunately, neighbors shared their anger and feuds as well. No family could keep a secret living in the close quarters. Communal life under Stalin destroyed any right to privacy.

Even so, Yeltsin apparently did not think much about

social condtions or politics as a young man. He despised the commune for the most part, yet accepted it as a fact of life. He developed an ability to endure bitter conditions, and learned to channel his frustration into hard work.

One benefit the communist nation did grant its citizens was the right to an education. Boris made the most of his schooling, nearly always achieving the highest marks in his class. He also demonstrated a natural ability to lead, earning annual election as class leader from the first grade on.

But a rebellious streak kept Yeltsin from becoming a perfect student. His conduct grades were usually among his lowest marks. After school, he often got into gang fights, and some foes thrashed him badly. "When two solid walls of opponents clashed head-on, however strong you might be, you would always end up with several bumps on your head," Yeltsin said.[5] Once, an enemy broke his nose with the wooden shaft from a cart. He bears the mark of that brawl to this day.

Boris saw himself as an adventurer. Often, he did not pay enough attention to the risks he and his friends took on their escapades. His determination to prove himself a leader sometimes tempted him to take the most dangerous risks in front of his little band. One such episode cost him two fingers on his left hand.

The incident happened during World War II, which

Russians call the Great Patriotic War. As a prank Boris organized a raid on a Soviet arsenal housed in an old church. He took it upon himself to play the commando, cutting through three layers of wire mesh and sneaking past a sentry to steal two grenades. Afterward, the boys traveled to a forest to test their new weapons. Yeltsin volunteered to test one of the grenades. He did not have much trouble persuading his band to stand a hundred yards away while he pounded the grenade on a rock. But he did not know enough to remove the fuse first.

The resulting explosion sent ripped flesh flying from his left hand, a wound so severe Boris fainted several times on the way to the hospital. When gangrene struck, the surgeons had no choice but to amputate two of his fingers.

One might think such a misadventure would have convinced the young Yeltsin to begin gauging his risks more carefully. Yet Boris continued to dare fate, time and again.

One of his strategies was to make life very uncomfortable for his foes, such as an unpopular teacher he considered both lazy and cruel. The teacher took pleasure in embarrassing her students, such as humiliating a boy in the presence of his girlfriend. She would also hit pupils with a heavy ruler, force them to stand in corners, or make them carry out her household chores, such as feeding her pig. Boris made up his mind that teacher would receive her own just punishment.

Just as he had with the grenade earlier, Boris threw aside all caution when he sought revenge for himself and his classmates. He unleashed his wrath on his primary school's graduation day.

Six hundred people watched as school officials handed out diplomas during the dignified ritual. The solemn event went well until Boris sprung his trap. He asked permission to address the crowd. Because he had earned high grades and demonstrated his leadership, school officials let him speak.

Boris started his address on a high and noble note. He congratulated most of his teachers for doing their jobs well, and for preparing their students for the future. Then he announced he wanted to speak of a teacher who did not deserve his praise. He told the shocked parents and faculty about her list of sins. Boris ended his stern lecture—an astonishing act in itself for a young student—with his opinion that the woman should never have been allowed to teach children. "She was a horror and I had to say what I had to say," Boris told a writer years later.[6]

The ceremony disintegrated; faculty and onlookers were outraged.

On the heels of this fiasco, Yeltsin acted in defiance again the next day. School officials told Boris' father they would not give his son a diploma. Instead, he would get a "wolf's ticket"—a certificate saying he had finished primary school. But with this, he could not advance his education anywhere in Russia.

Nikolai attempted to punish Yeltsin in the manner he had used many times before—with his strap. But Boris yanked the whip from his father's hand and refused to take the beating.

"That's enough," Boris said. "From now on, I'm going to educate myself." [7] His father backed down, and never again tried to whip his oldest son. Thus Boris ended one of the harsher ordeals of his youth.

Boris won his fight with the teacher as well. He refused to accept the school board's verdict, and fought it under the established rules of the system. He took his case to higher authority one step at a time, appealing first to the district and then the city board of education. Finally, he succeeded in getting a committee of inquiry to investigate his charges. This is how Boris Yeltsin first learned how to operate within a bureaucracy. It was excellent training for his later life in communist politics.

Boris had learned his first lesson on how to prevail in the communist world, for the party committee restored his diploma and fired the teacher from the school. To save face, it did give him an unsatisfactory grade in conduct—a slap on the wrist for a student who had turned his graduation ceremony into chaos.

Perhaps without knowing it, Boris had first tapped an inner resource which would fuel his success for the rest of his public life. He learned how to take a punch from the communist system, recover, and then use the rules to hit back. This is how he would survive later, despite the assaults of many enemies, and during times of nearly constant upheaval.

Boris did not return to the school that had expelled him. Instead, he went to Sverdlovsk's Pushkin School, a place he grew to love. At Pushkin, he found no lazy or inept teachers. All of them, he thought, were excellent.

At Pushkin, Boris blossomed as an athlete. He loved volleyball, and discovered he had a natural gift for the game. At times, he felt almost like he could control the ball at will. Like some American high school football quarterbacks, he tried to hone his instincts by sleeping with the ball. Other sports, too, held their lure. He sampled boxing, wrestling, skiing, gymnastics and track. But nothing could replace volleyball.

His confidence in athletics probably made him a little cocky. The summer after the ninth grade, he led a group of friends on an adventurous expedition through the Ural mountains. In the end, he found he could not have his way against nature as effortlessly as he did with a ball. The expedition nearly cost him and his friends their lives.

The goal of his band's quest was to find the source of a local river, the Yaiva. They knew it lay somewhere near the crest of the Urals, but its exact location was a mystery. They hiked for days. But soon ran out of food and began feeding on berries and mushrooms. For explorers who knew how to use it, the forest provided plenty to eat. Having traveled on such expeditions for many summers, Boris's band likely considered themselves experts in the woods. They slept in the open for the most part, occasionally making use of a deserted hut to bed down for the night.

And they succeeded in their mission. They found the source of the Yaiva river to be a natural hydrogen sulfide spring. They reveled in their accomplishment, not knowing how soon their triumph would turn into a nightmare.

On the journey home, weary from their long march, they decided to make their return a bit easier. In a small village, they worked out a trade with a cottage owner: all of their equipment for a flat-bottomed boat. They planned an easy homecoming, floating lazily down the Yaiva river.

Their ordeal began innocently enough. Glimpsing the mouth of a cave on a hillside, they could not resist the lure of one last, brief adventure. They moored their boat and went inside. But they had overestimated their skills as explorers.

In the dark, they soon found they had lost the light of the cave's mouth. They could not find their way back out, and could only keep going ahead until they came out on the other side of the hill.

Unlike the abundant forest they had left behind, a desolate wasteland lay outside the far mouth of the cave. The band trudged through miles of swampland, finding little edible vegetation and only stagnant water to drink. They strained the filthy water through a shirt and managed to get enough of it down to survive as they wandered, desperately lost, for nearly a week.

They finally found their way back to the boat. But by that time, they had become gravely ill from drinking swamp water. The first symptoms of deadly typhoid fever set in. Their faces flushed with fever, and they began passing out. Boris began feeling faint, but he struggled to remain alert. As the organizer of the expedition, he felt responsible. He remained on his feet as he loaded those who could not walk into the boat.

He forced himself to stay alert long enough to launch the boat. Then he too felt his senses begin to leave him, as he faded in and out of consciousness. When they finally passed under a railway bridge spanning the river banks, Boris realized the spot might mark their best chance of being found. He moored the boat, then passed out.

Boris's band did not know that search parties were already looking for them. A passerby spotted them, and they were driven back to town and taken to a hospital.

The hospital could offer little treatment for typhoid, and the boys spent another three months recovering. His friends decided they would skip the tenth grade—their last of secondary school—and complete it the following year. But Boris could not stand the idea of losing a year. He was too eager to go on to college at Ural Polytechnic Institute.

Boris got his books and studied at home. He studied hard and managed to persuade school officials to let him enter the tenth grade halfway through the year. Even then, catching up proved difficult. Boris did not finish the year with the high marks he usually earned, but he did get his diploma.

Before Yelsin was allowed to enter the Polytechnic, his stubborn grandfather placed one last obstacle in his path. The old man demanded that Boris pass a test to prove he was worthy of higher education. He made him build the family a bath house, a luxury it had never before enjoyed. Grandfather refused to do any of the work himself. Boris would have to cut the wood, carry it two miles to the site, and nail it together.

One might suspect Boris's grandfather had a more selfish reason in mind than testing his grandson's mettle. Nonetheless, Boris accepted the task, and went about it with his usual drive. When he finished the construction, his grandfather issued his solemn pronouncement: Boris had passed the test. He could now enter the university.

Boris made the pursuit of excellence in sports one of his first objectives at the Polytechnic. He became captain on the sports association, a job which sometimes made it hard to find time to study. Eventually, he made the city volleyball team. A year later, he worked his way to the senior league, playing on a team which competed with the twelve best in the nation. His athletic pursuits gave him a self-discipline he never lost, and contributed to his popularity on campus.

Boris became part of a tight clique of friends, six boys and six girls, which lasted well beyond his college years. Among the girls was Naya Girina. Bright and unpretentious, Naya tempered Boris's headstrong bravado and bluster. Soon they were more than friends.

The couple was slow to show their affection, however. In that era, boys were shy. They might kiss the girls on their cheeks in a comradely fashion, which was all Boris did at first. Then one night the two found themselves alone in an upstairs gallery of Urals Polytechnic entry hall. Only then did they share their first romantic kiss, almost two years after they had first met.

By this time, Boris had taken on the business of growing up as earnestly as if it were an assigned job. When his first year in college ended, he decided to spend his summer traveling around the country. He made the journey hobo-style, hopping trains by night. He had no money and only one set of clothes assembled from his athletic gear. He carried one clean shirt in a small leather suitcase, and only wore it when working odd jobs for food. A friend started the trip with him, but soon decided he did not care for life on the road, and left Boris to travel alone.

The Soviet police sometimes made life difficult for travelers like Boris. They would stop him and demand to know where he was going. He figured out a trick, however. When asked his destination, he gave the police the name of a nearby city, saying he was on his way to see his grand-mother.

The police would demand he be more specific: What street does she live on?

"Lenin Street," Boris would answer.[8] He knew that almost every city in the country had a street named after Vladimir Lenin, the founder of the Soviet Union. His ploy would usually result in his release.

He traveled to Moscow, Leningrad, and twenty other cities in a span of two months. Inside the city, he traveled to the best known public squares, then staked out a place in a park or other haven to sleep. He explored each city for a few days, sending postcards to his friends back home.

While hopping freights, he sometimes found himself among low companions. A group of released prisoners discovered him in a rail car one day. They had just received an enormous boon—the government had granted them amnesty. No doubt, some had been political prisoners, and had not deserved to be locked up in the first place. But, for the most part, they were a crude lot. One such group proposed a game of strip poker. Soon, Boris had lost everything except his underwear. The stakes for the last hand were high. If he lost, the ex-prisoners said, they would throw Boris off the train. But when Boris won the hand, the prisoners gave everything back to him—watch, hat, shirt and trousers. He wondered afterward if they had set him up for a joke all along. They proved good traveling companions over the long run, sharing food and tea with him.

On his return to the university, Boris dropped his happy-go-lucky lifestyle and regained an unstinting self-discipline. He worked long hours on the volleyball court, and studied hard as well.

During their last year at the Polytechnic, Boris and Naya found their love would be tested. When they learned that they would be assigned jobs in different provinces—Naya in Orenburg, Boris in Sverdlovsk—they made a pledge to wait a year before deciding whether to marry.

Meeting the requirements of graduation proved tough

Ural Polytechnical Institute, where Boris studied Civil Engineering.
(Sovfoto)

enough, even without the emotional demands of courtship. Boris learned to sleep less, as little as three or four hours a night. Once, when an attack of tonsillitis struck, he collapsed on the volleyball court. The doctors at the hospital ordered him to rest, but that was an order Yeltsin did not obey. Lying in bed was not for him, despite the doctor's warning he could do permanent damage to his heart.

Boris talked his loyal friends into assisting with a scheme to get out of the hospital. They helped him make a rope ladder, which he scaled down from the top floor. He went back to his parents' home, saying he wanted to recover there.

But it did not take long for him to begin sneaking back to the volleyball court. He began to train again, pacing himself for one minute, then two, then five. His body rallied under his own regimen. As graduation neared, he recovered well enough to play in a volleyball tournament. But, at the academic and athletic pace Yeltsin had set for himself, nothing came easily. He barely managed to study enough to finish a very difficult architectural paper on how to erect a television tower. Yet Boris earned a good grade, and his college career ended on a high note.

Boris has never forgotten the friends he made at the university. He still meets with them once a year, always for some sort of rough-and-tumble excursion, almost on the order of his childhood expeditions.

Major national issues did not intrude into Boris's life during his college years. He has never written, or said publicly, about how he felt in March of 1953 when dictator Joseph Stalin died. He did not show much interest in political affairs, and probably never guessed he would one day be a politician.

Upon graduation, Boris entered the work world the same way he had trekked into the Ural Mountains—mapping his course, confident of reaching his goal, and unconcerned about any dangers that might be around the next corner.

TWO

FACTORY BOSS

The summer of Boris's graduation, in 1955, was a golden time for the young man. Freed from the constraints of balancing his volleyball and his studies, he briefly enjoyed the life of a full-time athlete.

Boris boarded a train an hour after his last exam, and set off for the city of Tbilisi to play in the national volleyball championships. After the games, Boris traveled the country that summer, playing in tournaments.

In September, Boris reported for work at the Urals Heavy Pipe Construction Trust. In the communist system, he did not have any choice about where to work. He had been given the employment assignment upon graduation.

But Boris did have one choice regarding his career, and made what appeared to be a surprising decision. His superiors offered him a foreman's job, a customary reward for new university graduates. He turned it down, saying he wanted to learn the twelve basic trades of the construction industry from the bottom up, thereby earning the rank of foreman.

Yeltsin's choice might have seemed to be a noble sacrifice. In fact, he was exhibiting the same forward-looking shrewdness he was to show throughout his work and political career. He knew many of the "common sense" skills of jobs could not be taught in university classes. One had to learn them firsthand. Boris also understood the resentment some older workers would have at being bossed by a green 24-year-old. An old hand, with superior work experience, could have questioned his authority or even ridiculed him. Boris would have none of that.

So Boris joined the laborers, working his way through the twelve basic trades. He toiled one month on each job, in a routine that always started with him at the bottom of the heap. Naturally, his co-workers subjected him to rough joking. But they also befriended and helped him. He learned much about the character of the working class, knowledge that would later serve him well in politics.

Throughout his apprenticeship, Yeltsin kept his sense of self-control and pride. He stuck with his volleyball, playing on the city team. And he and Naya passed the test they had set for themselves during their lovestruck senior year at the Polytechnic.

Fate seemed to take a hand in the blossoming of their courtship. Exactly a year after their pledge, Yeltsin recalls, the regional volleyball tournament took place in Kuibyshev, near where Naya worked. They talked on the telephone, both so giddy they could hardly contain themselves. They promised to meet in the town square.

"All that night, we walked around the town together, talking about everything under the sun" Boris later wrote. "We recalled our student days and told each other everything that had happened over the past year. I just wanted to go on listening and listening to her, to go on looking at her day and night."[1]

The couple announced their wedding plans on a return trip to Sverdlovsk. They asked their friends from Urals Polytechnic to meet them at the rooming house where Boris lived. Their senior year had produced a crop of marriages, and Boris had helped organize many of his classmates' weddings through the Komsomol, or Communist youth group. His comrades happily returned the favor. At a reception of about 150 young people, the couple's friends sang an ode to the newlyweds, gave them a fake "newspaper" about the event and entertained them until dawn.

In the early days of their marriage, Boris took the opportunity to do something he has rarely done since—reflect quietly on his life. In the evenings, he and Naya would sit on the front porch of her parents' home, talking and wondering what the future held for them.

Life would never again be quite so idyllic for the couple. When they returned to Sverdlovsk, Naya began her career at the Institute of Waterways. As Boris worked his way through the industrial ranks, Naya also earned promotions. She became the chief engineer for one of the Institute's major projects, and managed both her job and household chores. In 1957, a little less than a year after their marriage, Naya gave birth to their first daughter. Although Boris had hoped for a boy, he was delighted by his firstborn, whom they named Lena. About two years later, Naya became pregnant again. Boris, still wanting a son, followed Russian folk traditions designed to insure the birth of a boy, such things as putting an ax and a hat under his pillow. But fate did not cooperate. Naya gave birth to another daughter, Tanya.

Boris dearly loved both his children, but later admitted he did not spend as much time with them as he should have. As Boris worked his way up the political ladder, most of the childrearing burden fell on Naya's shoulders. Boris did take over at times, however. When Naya fell ill with pneumonia,

Boris took Tanya by train to her grandmother's house. Tanya was used to being breastfed, something Boris could not provide. The child began to cry loudly on the train. Other passengers felt sympathetic to Boris's problem, but none of the suggestions they offered to soothe her worked. Finally, Boris tried his own last-ditch method. He opened his shirt and let her suck on his chest for warmth and psychological comfort.

"Everyone chuckled," Boris wrote later. "The women on the train laughed almost until they cried. 'See, he fooled her,' they said."[2] But the trick worked. Perhaps it was the warmth, or Boris' heartbeat, but Tanya settled down.

Boris' uncomfortable train trip was only one of many trials the young couple faced during their early years of marriage. Both worked difficult jobs, and some of Boris' close brushes with danger in the workplace threatened to end his career before it started.

Despite the strength he'd acquired through athletics, Yeltson sometimes found pushing a wheelbarrow of liquid concrete along high scaffolding more than he could handle. Several time he tumbled from the narrow beam, wheelbarrow and all. Luckily, he always escaped serious injury.

A truck driver's life also carried hazards, Boris learned. He got the scare of his young life when he stalled on a railroad track in an old truck carrying a load of concrete.

As the engine died, he heard a train thundering toward him. Desperately, he engaged the starter, which turned the engine just enough to jerk the old truck forward a few feet at a time. By the time he leap-frogged the truck several times, the train was bearing down on him at full speed. The engineer must have shared Yeltsin's panic, for he blew the whistle and hit the brakes, even though he was too close to stop.

The truck cleared the track just in time. Yeltsin climbed from the cab and sat down on the ground for a long time, gasping for breath. The desire to avoid losing the truck, he later wrote, had nearly cost him his life.

A mistake as a crane operator put Yeltsin through another terrifying ordeal, one with a bit of humor in it, considering that he survived. While helping build an apartment house, Yeltsin parked his crane for the night and went home. He did not realize he had neglected one important detail.

He did not have far to walk home, for he and Naya shared an apartment next door. A windy storm struck that night and Boris woke in the middle of it. He looked out the window. In horror, he watched as the crane started slowly rolling down its track.

Boris had been guilty of a beginner's mistake. He had either forgotten, or did not know, he was supposed to lock the crane in place with small hooks that latched it to the track. Boris dashed into the downpour and raced across the construction lot. He scrambled into the cab, and released the jib—the crane's projecting arm—so the wind would not push it like a sail. He threw the motor into reverse. But the crane continued to slide down the track.

Finally, it stopped. He climbed down, secured the crane with the hooks, and slogged through the mud home, where he did not sleep another wink. In the weeks ahead, he suffered a recurring nightmare—reliving the scene, only with an ending that brought him crashing to the ground inside the crane.

Yeltsin's supervisors gave him grades for his work that were not always as high as he wished. Yet, he did well enough to be judged a professional in each of the trades he sampled. Returning to the Urals Heavy Pipe plant, Boris took on the foreman's job with a secure authority which came from experience. He no longer had to worry about someone berating him as an untested novice.

Some of the workers may have wished he had kept one of his temporary trades, because Yeltsin did not hesitate to push his crews. His superiors discovered that he always met deadlines. He was the classic example of the boss who drives his workers hard, himself harder, and many others crazy. Still, he had learned how to create a rapport with people, and many of the Urals Heavy Pipe workers liked him.

Other people, though, despised him. Boris did not worry about making enemies; in fact, he felt it was sometimes necessary. When he decided a group of convicts who worked at Urals Heavy Pipe made more in wages than they were entitled, he simply slashed their pay. He reaped the full fury from that decision in short order. A bull of a man from the convict crew charged into his office, brandishing an ax.

"Are you going to pay us at the proper rate like they always paid us before you came along, you puppy?" the convict asked.

"No," Boris said. In that case, the convict yelled, he would just smash Boris's skull.

Yeltsin refused to yield, even when the big man raised the ax over his head. Instead, he bellowed "Get out!" so loudly the command echoed off the walls of the small office. [3] His booming voice, later to prove useful in speeches, saved him that day. The startled convict lowered the ax, turned and slumped out of the office.

Going wherever Urals Heavy Pipe sent him, solving technical problems efficiently and wielding his authority without hesitation, Yeltsin gained prestige with his bosses. But he struggled against the intractable problems built into Soviet industry of the 1950s and 1960s. Even Premier Nikita Khrushchev, who had succeeded Stalin as the most powerful man in the Soviet world, grumbled about the inefficiency of the USSR's heavy industries.

Communism had removed the incentive for workers to care about what they made or built. The state, at least in theory, owned almost all property. Many construction projects came to completion with flaws caused by slipshod practices. Why should the individual worker care? He or she would not receive any of the benefits that derived from doing an excellent, or even a good, job. It was easier to simply go through the motions.

Boris discovered an astonishing mistake, for example, when trying to complete construction of a half-finished mill. Days from the deadline, he was told that a walkway intended to connect two wings of the building had never been built. Someone had simply lost the architectural plans. A company in a Western economy would have driven itself into bankruptcy by such absurd errors, but they were common in the Soviet Union. In addition, most workers cared little about production quotas or deadlines. Many had grown up on farms, where time is measured by the changing of the seasons instead of a factory clock. "Communism reinforced the native Russian disrespect for time because workers cannot be fired and there is no incentive to do things on time." wrote one American who studied in Russia.[4]

Boris solved his particular problem, not by pushing workers, but by pushing the other bosses. He held a long session with engineers and lit a fire under the project heads. By six the next morning, crews started pouring the asphalt for the walkway. Once again, Yeltsin met his deadline.

In the process, Boris earned a promotion to chief construction engineer. And by doing so, he found himself head to head with other enemies, as Yeltsin did at almost every crossroad in his life.

Yeltsin fought frequently with his boss, a short-tempered general manager named Nikolai Sitnikov. Their spats sometimes bordered on comedy. When they argued during business trips, Sitnikov would stop the car in the countryside and insist Yeltsin get out. Of course, Yeltsin refused. Who would set out walking from the middle of nowhere? But Sitnikov would sometimes wait as long as an hour before giving up. In the office, their fights would turn physical. The two would grab chairs and circle one another like drunks brawling in a bar.

The quarrels finally reached the breaking point when Sitnikov officially reprimanded Yeltsin for the seventeenth time in one year. Just before the year ended, Yeltsin marched into Sitnikov's office and threw the printed reprimands onto his superior's desk. "The next time you issue a reprimand in the new year, I shall kick up an almighty row," Boris said. "I'm warning you."[5] Sitnikov took the challenge. He wrote Yeltsin up for missing New Year's Day, an official holiday, but one the boss insisted Boris should have worked.

Yeltsin appealed to Party officials, who forced Sitnikov to take back the rebuke. Even then, the battle was not over. Sitnikov accused Yeltsin of accounting errors and dragged him into court. Again, Boris won. The judge ruled in Yeltsin's favor and reprimanded his boss. But Boris' victory gained him another enemy—a company accountant who had used bogus figures to back up Sitnikov. The accountant had shared in the judge's stinging rebuke. He wanted revenge, and soon got his chance. He attacked Boris when he applied for membership in the Communist Party in 1961.

Boris Yeltsin has written little about why he joined the Party. But any ambitious person who desired to move up in government simply had to be a Party member. Also, the new leader of the Party, and the Soviet Union, had made it safer to rise through the ranks than it had been under Joseph Stalin. Although often ruthless, Nikita Khrushchev ruled with far less bloodshed than had Stalin. Khrushchev even denounced Stalin's crimes during a famous speech in 1956. Even the men in Stalin's handpicked inner circle were not safe from his terror, Khrushchev revealed. He reported that Stalin had labeled many of his associates "enemies of the people" so he could get away with "the most cruel repression . . . against anyone who in any way disagreed with Stalin . . . the only proof of guilt used. . . was the 'confession' of the accused himself... secured through physical pressure."[6] By "physical pressure," Khrushchev meant torture.

Relations between the United States and the Soviet Union did not improve much during Khrushchev's era. Both continued to threaten the other during the "Cold War." It was a period of international tension that occasionally flared into wars, such as in Vietnam and in Korea, and in showdowns such as the Cuban Missile Crisis of 1962. But inside the Soviet Union, fear lessened. Khrushchev gave more freedom to artists, journalists and writers, though still much less than that in a democracy. He also made it safer to seek promotion to political office.

Still, becoming a Party member was not easy. The organization allowed only a select few to join. The person who wanted to enlist had to be nominated by a current member. The Communist Party carefully checked the background of would-be members, looking for any character stains or past deeds which would disqualify them. If none were found, the candidate was subjected to an intense face-to-face interview filled with tough questions to test the applicant's knowledge of Communism. It was during his interrogation that Boris' enemy, the accountant, tried to trick him.

"On which page of which volume of Marx's *Capital* does

Nikita Khrushchev (AP/Wide World)

he refer to commodity-money relationships?" the accountant demanded. Karl Marx was the 19th-century philosopher and author who had created the theory of communism. The book *Das Kapital* was one of his most famous works.

"Volume II, page 387," Boris answered quickly.[7]

Yeltsin had made up the answer on the spot, knowing the questioner did not know the answer to his absurd query any more than Yeltsin did. The accountant fell for the bluff, and even complimented Yeltsin on his knowledge of Marx.

As a new party member, Boris was awarded a job at another, larger industrial complex. Thus he was rid of Sitnikov, but not of personal skirmishes. He made enemies at every stop on the road throughout his long march to power. His foes often acted ruthlessly—and so did he. Almost always, he eventually prevailed, by using the system itself as a weapon.

Boris learned that friendly relations with common workers were as useful as alliances with party officials. Yeltsin enjoyed a particular popularity with women factory crews. He would pitch in on their night shifts, painting and hanging wallpaper with them. The women admired him greatly for it. It was a clever strategy for a manager who was often considered overly tough. He added to his popularity by devoting attention to little things generally ignored by management. Adding mirrors in the bathrooms, and handing out free dress material as a reward for good work, considerably improved the company's relation with the women employees.

Boris tried to strike a balance between his demanding, driven personality and his respect for worker's rights. He believed good performances should be rewarded, but indignantly renounced laziness, waste and sloppy work habits. Yeltsin himself worked long hours, slept less than most of his peers, and even played hard, usually in some athletic endeavor, during his rare spare time.

Boris frequently writes of his progress through the Communist Party as though he only grudgingly submitted to promotion to higher political rank. But, by now a Party member, he eagerly snatched up his first political job. After fourteen years in industry, high Communist officials rewarded him with an offer to head the section of the provincial committee that arranged construction. Indeed, he knew the offer for his first job as a government official was coming, because he had worked many hours for the party in his off-time to insure that it did.

Yeltsin later downplayed his desire to enter politics, saying merely that he was "satisfied" with the job, and enjoyed the higher salary. Yet he was probably even more satisfied at the opportunity to try out the management skills he had mastered on the job in the political arena.

For a man such as Boris, who knew the system, opportunities for power on the national stage were without limit. But the battles would be fiercer, and the climb tougher, as he would soon find out.

THREE

PROVINCE CHIEF

In the autumn of 1976, Boris was taking a two-week course at the Academy of Social Sciences in Moscow when, one day, the official teaching the course announced that a powerful man in the party had summoned Boris Yeltsin. The announcement awed the other students, as it did Yeltsin.

The teacher had one question for Boris: Did Yeltsin think he could handle a more important job? Yeltsin answered yes, and soon found himself being escorted through the Kremlin, the absolute center of power in the Soviet Union.

An aide waiting in an anteroom told him he was expected. Then the door opened and Yeltsin walked into the presence of the most powerful man in Russia—President Leonid Brezhnev. Brezhnev had come to power with the overthrow of Nikita Khrushchev in 1964.

Brezhnev, a burly man with dark hair and heavy eye-brows, sat at the end of a long table. He rose to greet Yeltsin. Bustling through the formalities, Brezhnev quickly adopted a joking tone.

"So he's decided to assume power in Sverdlovsk province, has he?" Brezhnev asked one of the men who had escorted Yeltsin.

The lesser official replied that Yeltsin did not yet know why he had been brought to the Kremlin.

"How can he not know, when he's decided to assume power?" Brezhnev jokingly demanded.[1] The leader was having a bit of fun at Yeltsin's expense. No one in the Soviet Union merely "decided" to assume power. Brezhnev's joshing suggested Yeltsin was pulling off a coup, in which case he would have more likely found himself facing a firing squad than exchanging jokes with the Russian president.

Having pulled Boris' leg for a while, Brezhnev then got to the point. He informed Yeltsin the Politburo had recommended him to be the new first secretary of the Sverdlovsk's provincial committee. The new job would mean that Boris would be the most powerful man in his home province. Promoting Boris meant that the second secretary, who normally would have been next in line, had been bypassed.

Yeltsin accepted the new position without hesitation, assuring the president that he would give the job all the energy and dedication he had. Brezhnev then told Yeltsin it would take a while for him to be confirmed by the Central Committee, the governing body for the Soviet Union, because the Committee had already concluded its elections for that year.

With the important business out of the way, Brezhnev returned to the locker room-style humor with which he had first greeted his new appointee. He saw that Yeltsin's lapel lacked the badge of a deputy of the Supreme Soviet. Each republic had a Supreme Soviet which was its highest council, and Moscow's Supreme Soviet was the most powerful in the nation.

"Aren't you a deputy?" Brezhnev asked. Yeltsin replied that he was.

"What sort of deputy is he?" Brezhnev asked the others.

With a straight face, Yeltsin replied: "Of the provincial sort."[2]

Brezhnev and his aides had a good laugh on that one. Provincial deputies did not count for much in the corridors from which Russia's global power flowed. But Brezhnev made it clear he stood solidly behind Yeltsin as the meeting ended. He ordered the officials to see that Yeltsin was quickly confirmed at the next plenum, one of the standard meetings of the Party committees.

Leonid Brezhnev (AP/Wide World)

Yeltsin's acceptance speech before the Committee promised that his administration would center around the people's needs. He told the delegates the workers would only do their best for the country, and the party, when they were treated well.

Although he had good words for the workers, Boris was tough on the bureaucrats who now were under his command. Yeltsin took an ax to the ranks of the Sverdlovsk hierarchy, chopping out anyone he deemed inefficient or difficult to work with. Next, he selected the most able people to work closely with him.

Once his handpicked staff was in place, Boris allowed them some degree of freedom, as long as they matched his furious pace. This included letting them criticize him to his face—but only in closed meetings. Arguments broke out sometimes, but none that threatened the reforms he had planned.

Even Boris' vacations involved work. He and his lieutenants took public holidays together, accompanied by their wives. Boris decreed that all of his staff would play sports to stay in shape. "In Sverdlovsk, I had dragged practically the whole regional party office staff out on the volleyball court, and then they started liking volleyball so much they could not be chased off the court," Boris wrote later.[3]

Boris promised to visit all 45 towns in Sverdlovsk every two years, along with its 63 townships. He made good on the pledge. In party halls, public assemblies, farms and fields, Yeltsin made himself known. He especially liked to meet farmers and workers, thus playing the role of both good Communist and common man.

In public meetings, Yeltsin encouraged people to air their concerns. Yet many were reluctant to talk freely. People still remembered what happened to those who had protested during the days of Stalin. Most citizens did not expect much to change under any provincial secretary chosen by Brezhnev.

Unfortunately, the people were right to a great extent. The system was thoroughly corrupt, with bribes, falsified wage sheets and work quotas, and a myriad of production problems. These things were not solely Breznev's fault; they had also been common under other leaders. But Brezhnev paid even less attention to the corruption, and the problems worsened as he grew older.

In his work in Sverdlovsk and other provinces, Yeltsin discovered officials who had grown so disillusioned that they "forgot" to carry out some orders from Moscow. If he ever did the same, Yeltsin has not admitted it. But there were some Politburo orders he questioned, and at least one he considered repulsive.

Yeltsin had to fight daily against the inertia of the Soviet system. Later, he described a typical example of the way he had to do business with the Soviet president. Boris wanted a subway system built for Sverdlovsk. He made the call to Brezhnev and was granted a meeting on Thursday, the last day of Brezhnev's four-day work week. But others had warned him how badly Brezhnev's concentration had deteriorated. So Yeltsin arrived with the document already drafted.

After they had talked for a few minutes, Yeltsin made his proposal. Brezhnev accepted it without taking the time to consider the idea fully.

"Just dictate to me what I should write," he told Yeltsin. So Yeltsin dictated words to the effect that the Politburo now ordered the building of the Sverdlovsk subway.

Brezhnev handed the paper back to Yeltsin. But Yeltsin refused to take the chance his subway order would get lost in the bureaucratic mess the Soviet government had become.

"No, you should call your aide," he told Brezhnev, who then meekly did what he was told by the man he had once so jokingly patronized. When the aide appeared, Yeltsin told him what needed to be done in order to make the act official. Now confident that the order would go through, Yeltsin exchanged farewells with the president.[4]

Boris later wrote of his dismay at Brezhnev's mental deterioration, and the resulting decay of the nation. "Granted, as a result of that signature a good deed was done and Sverdlovsk soon received permission to build a metro," Yeltsin wrote. "But how many of the rogues and cheats, indeed plain criminals, who surrounded Brezhnev exploited him for their own dishonest purposes? How many resolutions or decrees did he calmly, unthinkingly sign, bringing riches to a few and suffering to many?"[5]

Even as Brezhnev's hold on power and his own faculties declined, Yeltsin's importance grew. So did his ambition. He has always proclaimed a contempt for party officials who profit from their personal niches in the Soviet Union's massive bureaucratic network. Russians sarcastically call such people "apparatchiks," people who work like cogs in the Party apparatus. In his own writings, Boris describes himself as an tireless foe of yes-men, a rebel against the corrupt and comfortable hierarchy.

Yet his critics have charged Yeltsin was the perfect party machine politician. He always focused on his rise to power. He rarely took any step not calculated to enhance his political standing, opponents say, even while proclaiming the well-being of the common worker as his top concern.

The real Yeltsin is probably somewhere between these two extremes. Certainly, he has always loved power and has admitted that it intoxicated him. No doubt he wanted his work in Sverdlovsk to earn favorable reviews in Moscow. But it is also hard to believe that he was not sincere in his empathy for the working class, after his harsh childhood on a collective farm. If one chooses to criticize Yeltsin for ambition, it might be best to keep in mind that many an American politician—or statesman—pursued political ends in just as single minded a fashion.

Even if Yeltsin was only a successful *apparatchik*, the Soviet system provided few other routes to success during his early career. The same could be said of Mikhail Gorbachev, who became General Secretary of the Communist Party and

President of the Soviet Union. But when the two first met, they held identical jobs.

Gorbachev had also earned his position by being a good communist. He was the first secretary of the province of Stavropol when he had his first conversation with Yeltsin by telephone. The two worked well together at first, trading supplies and goods between their provinces. They were the same age, though of different backgrounds. Gorbachev had studied at Moscow State University, the most elite school in the Soviet Union, while Yeltsin labored at Ural Polytechnic. Unlike Yeltsin, who had begun his career in industry, Gorbachev had spent his whole working life as a party official. He had joined the Communist Party ten years before Yeltsin.

In keeping with his rapid ascent, Gorbachev earned another promotion before Yeltsin did. In 1978, he was elected Secretary of the Central Committee of Agriculture. This worked to Yeltsin's advantage as well, since agriculture continued to be a problem in Sverdlovsk. He could use all the help Gorbachev could offer.

Like Yeltsin, Gorbachev enjoyed meeting common people. Once while Gorbachev was visiting Stavropol farms, an old shepherd who had known Gorbachev for years greeted him by his nickname and with a friendly bear hug. "Hey, Misha! Have you eaten?" the shepherd asked. To the surprise of

Gorbachev's aides, the first secretary of the province joined the shepherd in his hut for a bowl of soup.[6]

Despite this shared trait, Gorbachev's personality differed from Yeltsin's in many ways. Whenever the two met, for example, the amiable Gorbachev would embrace him. Yeltsin found this gesture uncomfortable. But the two worked together well. Yeltsin admired Gorbachev's honesty and his quickness to speak his mind. Yet he secretly held qualms about Gorbachev's plans to improve Soviet agriculture. Yeltsin did not think his counterpart sufficiently understood the problems.

The gap between the two widened when a public quarrel erupted between Yeltsin and one of Gorbachev's deputies. A commission arrived in Sverdlovsk one day to check on farming progress. The report noted both successes and failures. Yeltsin agreed with some of the failures listed, but disagreed with others.

At a meeting Yeltsin stood up and said he agreed with most of the report, but that much of it was based on mistakes made by Gorbachev's employees. There followed an uncomfortable silence. When Gorbachev's lieutenant attempted to defend the report, Yeltsin lost his temper, and the two men argued loudly before the assembled officials.

Later, Gorbachev called Yeltsin to his office in Moscow, where Yeltsin still refused to accept the report's conclusions.

Gorbachev cautioned Yeltsin to re-consider, and to avoid a protracted conflict, but Yeltsin refused to give in.

The two officials, whose future conflicts would be much more public, had had their first battle. The resentment would linger. Yeltsin would never again totally trust Gorbachev's gestures toward friendship. But he did accept their working alliance. The two very different men shared the knowledge that the Soviet system was suffering a serious decline.

But even if the system were in decay, there were certain orders even a man as independent as Boris Yeltsin could not disobey. A reminder of the Soviet government's crushing power appeared in Boris' office one day. It arrived in a letter stamped "Secret."

FOUR

SOLDIER FOR
THE PARTY

While Sverdlovsk's citizens slept, Boris Yeltsin's bulldozers rumbled onto the site of the one of the Soviet Union's
most infamous landmarks.

It was the Ipatiev house, a place with a grisly history. On
July 17, 1918, the soldiers of the Communist revolution had
turned it into a slaughterhouse for Czar Nicholas II, the last
Russian Monarch, and his family.

The revolutionaries, too, had done their work by night.
They had taken the czar's family, held for months as
hostages at the Ipatiev house, and escorted them to the cellar.
There a firing squad shot them dead—the czar, his wife and
five children. They carried the bodies into the countryside
and buried them in unmarked graves.

Even by 1976, it was not an event in which modern Soviet

leaders placed much pride. But the Ipatiev house fascinated citizens. Its very infamy attracted both pilgrims and curiosity seekers. The politicians in Moscow, of course, did not like the idea of legions of tourists visiting the site of a Soviet atrocity. The solution to the problem came from the Politburo, a group which acted like the board of directors for the Central Committee. The Politburo ran the country, and few dared disobey its commands, even on tasks as unpleasant as the one it now handed Boris Yeltsin. The Politburo decided to put an end to the legend of the Ipatiev house in its usual fashion—it would bury the ugly past.

This was the secret message the ruling body had sent Yeltsin. In a closed session, the Politburo had voted to have the Ipatiev house razed by night—and Yeltsin was to carry out the task.

As Yeltsin knew, Party propagandists for decades had attempted to smooth over the story of the executions. But he could also see that many ordinary people had seen through the propaganda. They came in hordes to stand in the yard, to peer through the windows. Nothing stopped the pilgrims from coming. Yeltsin had read the true story of the massacre in the archives of the Urals committee. "It made painful reading," he later wrote.[1]

Even so, the curiosity about the house did not bother Yeltsin. Some interest in such an historical place seemed normal to him. He had more important things to concern himself with, and thought the Politburo did too.

Boris was mistaken. When he announced the Politburo's orders to his associates in the provincial party bureau, a heated argument ensued. His colleagues wanted to refuse the task. But Yeltsin argued that he had no choice. It was one thing to "forget" to carry out a minor order, as officials sometimes did, but another thing altogether to defy a command of this magnitude. If the Ipatiev house were left standing, the Politburo would certainly notice.

So, the bulldozers carried out their work. The walls of the Ipatiev house came crashing down in the darkness. The next day, crews poured asphalt over the site. Now the house itself lay in an unmarked grave.

Yeltsin later said the incident cast a shadow over his conscience, and that considered the Politburo order an atrocity. However, Yeltsin was no serious rebel in those days. In fact, he made friends with chiefs of the KGB, a secret police agency which had a history of many atrocities. The image of the secret police had changed much since Stalin's time, when its agents would drag people from their beds to face torture or prison. The shrewd directors of the KGB had done what they could to erase the memory of Stalin's secret police, portraying the agency as the nation's protector against American spies. Russian television audiences of the

1960s watched James Bond-style KGB superheroes in adventure shows.

But Boris was not interested in the KGB's image; he needed to make connections with the powerful people who ran the organization. With that goal in mind, he courted every ally who could help him in his work—and could perhaps further his ambitions.

A good example of how Boris used his political skills and contacts within the Communist Party came into play when he had the opportunity to destroy a Stalin-era holdover he personally hated—the collective huts where he and his family had shivered and starved for most of his childhood. When the Politburo passed a measure demanding the huts to be torn down, Boris was eager to do so. Yet, as usual, the decision to do away with the huts became tangled in the bureaucratic maze which so often stalled Soviet attempts at progress. The tenants of the huts could not be moved to modern housing for another ten years. Yeltsin knew the hut-dwellers had grown too impatient to wait so long. He had once shared their poor living conditions, and he now understood their frustration.

When he tried to speed up the schedule, Boris hit another roadblock. To move the people immediately would exceed the entire building capacity of the province for a year. Also, the hut dwellers were not the only Sverdlovsk citizens waiting for decent housing. The waiting list was long, and included war veterans and many people with disabilities.

Yeltsin considered the prospect of "freezing" the current waiting list and first moving those living in the huts into the new housing. After all, they had endured the greater misery.

But moving the people in huts first would guarantee not only the wrath of those on the current list, but of the factory managers as well. It was part of the managers' jobs to find housing for their employees. If they did not, they would face the anger of their workers and a drop in workplace morale.

Yeltsin decided in favor of the hut dwellers, and froze the waiting list for everybody else. Then he braced for the hail of criticism to come.

The first step in his plan was to make sure his own bosses in Moscow knew what he was about to do, and that they would stand by him through the ordeal. In short, he asked Party leaders to ignore complaints from factory managers about their workers ending up on the "frozen list" for new housing. Ignoring complaints had become an art in Moscow by then, and party officials quickly agreed.

Yeltsin had not been mistaken in expecting the managers to rain curses on his head. But his powerful Moscow allies sealed the door on those protests, and Boris won his fight over housing with the help of these higher-ups in the Communist Party.

In leveling the huts, Boris had also destroyed a symbol of old-style communism which had haunted him. The man who had cuddled on the floor with the family goat for warmth in the collective huts during his impoverished youth had sent such hovels crashing to the ground, at least in his own province. It seemed he could change the old communist world with his own hands.

Yet, he grew concerned that he was becoming to much like the other party bosses he was growing to despise. Later, he admitted he wished he had "lost" the top secret order to demolish the death house of Russia's last czar. But he had not, and he also found himself adopting the bullying style of many Soviet leaders in party meetings. Yeltsin never minded giving orders, but he grew weary of having to use threats to enforce discipline. But it was what the system demanded. More and more, Yeltsin began to think that the problem was in the system itself.

Yeltsin was not the only official who grew impatient as Brezhnev's hold over the Soviet Union slowly slipped away. Gorbachev became so depressed over his inability to make Moscow listen to his ideas that he told an aide he did not know whether he could stand to go to work in the morning. While Brezhnev withered away, the country stagnated, and many Communist Party officials, like Gorbachev and Yeltsin, complained.

Average citizens also grumbled. Although government supplies and rations were limited, goods flowed freely on the illegal black market. Many people disregarded the law. They bought everything from toothpaste to caviar from illegal vendors, and did not worry about the penalties.

Brezhnev accepted this because the black market provided goods the system could not produce. But did Brezhnev also realize how bitter most Soviet citizens were toward him? Citizens who had thrilled to the exploits of television KGB agents—even though the secret police may have terrorized members of their own families during the 1930s—turned the channel when they saw Brezhnev's face.

Boris found himself growing frustrated as the country's highest leader diminished in stature. He did not like the black market, the bribes, the forgotten orders, the system's lies, nor the tangled path it took to accomplish a simple goal. After ten years in office under Brezhnev, Yeltsin began to see his once-promising job as provincial secretary running into a dead end.

FIVE

THE CALL
TO MOSCOW

On the evening of April 3, 1985, Boris Yeltsin finished a work day in his typical frenzied fashion. He and his advisors grappled much of the afternoon with the grim forecast of a spring drought, and possible solutions. When the meeting ended, Yeltsin got in his car and took a tour of Sverdlovsk food shops.

His circle had decided to delay the planting of certain crops; members now wanted to consult agricultural experts. But first things first. Before talking to the experts, Yeltsin wanted to see whether store shelves contained enough food reserves for a delay to be imposed. His wife Naya had already warned him of grumblings about food shortages she had heard on her job.

"I do go to the grocery stores in the center of town and

there are all sorts of things missing," she told Boris. "And that's in the center. What about the suburbs?"[1]

Boris found some meat, cheese and eggs in the government controlled shops, but wondered if they would be enough if a drought did strike. He returned home, still pondering how to deal with his province's predicament.

Little did he realize Moscow would lift the problem from his shoulders before the night ended. Yeltsin had long since established himself as a warrior for the regime, even when it called for unpleasant deeds and messy political battles. Now Moscow would repay him, in its own fashion.

Yeltsin's office phone rang soon after he arrived. A party official gave him the good news. Yeltsin had been promoted; he would go to Moscow to join the Central Committee as head of construction.

But the news was not so good to Yeltsin, as he later wrote. He thought "two seconds" about the offer, then said no. He fretted over the call and his future the whole day, knowing his refusal would not end the matter.

It's hard to imagine what went through Yeltsin's mind that next night; his statements about inner feelings sometimes contradict one another. The Central Committee job was well-suited to his experience. Yet he no doubt felt some sorrow, perhaps even fear, at the notion of leaving Sverdlovsk. He had grown up there and knew the province's people well.

He had handled Sverdlovsk's worst emergencies and headed up its greatest achievements. He had overseen the building of a 312-mile highway linking its industrial cities. He had improved crop production and forged a bond with the people.

What he may have feared most was losing his status as the top leader of an organization. If he took the Central Committee post, he would have bosses—lots of them. His power to make decisions quickly, and on his own, would disappear.

On top of that, Yeltsin shared some of the resentment his people felt for Moscow. When he visited the city, he keenly disliked the patronizing attitude many of the nation's leaders showed toward the provinces. Moscow was the showplace of Russia, receiving legions of foreign tourists every year. The city not only was the home of beautiful buildings and public landmarks, but its stores were well-stocked with food and clothing. Naturally, Moscow's prosperity provoked envy from citizens in other areas of the country. And Muscovites resented the way visiting outsiders clogged lines at shops, grappling for a share of goods so rare elsewhere. Though many provincials considered Moscow dwellers arrogant snobs, many a farmer or factory worker dreamed of sending their children to live in the great city which offered so much.

They knew, as Yeltsin did, that most paths to success ran only through Moscow.

The next morning, another call from the capital came, as Yeltsin probably knew it would. An even higher-ranking official repeated the offer. Again Yeltsin refused, citing the unsolved problems he would have to leave behind in Sverdlovsk. Then the caller made it clear that the proposal was no longer an offer — it was a command from the Party.

That was the end of it. The decision had been made for Boris. Nine days later, Yeltsin found himself behind the desk of an office at the Central Committee.

Boris felt a little lost and, unusually for him, a bit frightened as well. As a young man riding the rails, big cities had excited him. But it was another thing altogether to be a 54-year-old man with a family, trying to make a new start.

At first he was alone in Moscow. Naya and their oldest daughter Lena had stayed behind, with plans to join him later. He took an apartment in a rough, noisy section of the city, saying he did not really care where he lived.

He tackled his loneliness the only way he knew how, by throwing himself into his work. Days stretched from eight in the morning to midnight. Some of his close deputies kept up the pace with him, but other subordinates rejected such a grind. Boris did not demand the furious pace from all his underlings, but did not tolerate slackness either.

The Committee's construction work projects helped ease his depression in the beginning. He was in his element dealing with managers, factories and quotas. If he only had to deal with his assigned task, he might have found his place quickly in Moscow. But politics played a greater role in the capital than in the provinces. Leaders near his own office changed the course of the nation with strokes of their pens.

Yeltsin liked his new proximity to power, but he hated the price he had to pay. In Sverdlovsk, he had felt almost like a king. Here in Moscow, he felt more like one of a king's minor counselors.

Keeping silent under rules that irked him had never been one of Yeltsin's skills. During a lecture by one of his Central Committee bosses, he broke ranks with his colleagues. While they faithfully scribbled down every word from the man's mouth, Yeltsin jotted down only headings for major ideas.

It surprised his instructor, used to seeing his pupils write furiously for fear of missing a word. After glaring at Yeltsin off and on for the better part of the session, he asked if Boris had any questions, any areas of confusion he could clear up.

"No, I've remembered everything," Yeltsin replied. His instructor, wisely letting the challenge pass, simply continued his lesson plan.[2]

At times, Yeltsin's prickly personality annoyed his superiors, but his stubbornness was part of an inner drive that enabled him to succeed with even the toughest project. It helped him to survive the in-fighting of Moscow's circle of power.

In time, his enemies learned they could never count Yeltsin out. Perhaps his toughness came from his years as an athlete. He was like a boy who loses a fight on the school yard, then comes back an hour later wanting to fight again.

By the time Yeltsin traveled to Moscow, Mikhail Gorbachev had ascended to the rank of General Secretary of the Central Committee, the highest office of the Communist Party. Gorbachev was not yet an enemy of Yeltsin's; despite past disagreements, their relationship remained cordial. But they were fast approaching a crossroads in their friendship. Yeltsin did not like the fact that Gorbachev preferred to do business with him by phone, rather than face to face. He took it as a snub.

Also, Boris could not suppress his resentment that Gorbachev had achieved such a high rank, after the two had held nearly identical jobs as province chiefs. Gorbachev's Stavropol, after all, was poorer than Sverdlovsk. The fact that Gorbachev had joined the Communist Party ten years before him did not alter Yeltsin's feelings.

Gorbachev had worked very hard to become leader of the Soviet Union. He had taken dangerous risks as well. He allied himself in the early 1980s with Yuri Andropov, a high-ranking Soviet official who dared to wage a power struggle against President Leonid Brezhnev. When Brezhnev died in 1982, Andropov rose to power, and Gorbachev became his right-hand man. After only 15 months in office, Andropov died, and was replaced by another ailing old man, Constantin Chernenko. When Chernenko died in 1985, Gorbachev became the General Secretary of the Soviet Union. The Soviet Union's new leader brought a fresh approach and radical ideas to the country, some of which Boris would embrace enthusiastically.

At first, Yeltsin had his hands full just adjusting to life in the capital. His mood improved when his wife Naya joined him, along with two granddaughters, his eldest daughter Lena and son-in-law Valera. His youngest daughter, Tanya, already lived in the city. The reunited family at first shared the apartment in the run-down neighborhood, but when Yeltsin was confirmed in his new position, the government offered them a *dacha,* or mansion. In fact, it was the home Gorbachev had lived in until his elevation to general secretary.

Yeltsin's first priority was the same as when he had been made chief of Sverdlovsk province ten years before—he wanted to meet the people. Yeltsin was a populist, a man who liked to "press the flesh" in the style of American politicians.

His style would not have worked had he been an official in Stalin's time. But in the new Soviet Union Gorbachev was building, Yeltsin's time had come.

Gorbachev had introduced two new words to the vocabulary of the Soviet Union—*glasnost* and *perestroika*. *Glasnost* means "openness." It is similar to what Americans call "freedom of speech," Gorbachev wanted a government where not only officials, but writers, journalists and ordinary citizens felt free to speak their minds. *Perestroika* means "reform." Gorbachev's main target of reform was the relationship between the government and the Communist Party. Before Gorbachev's rise to the office of General Secretary, government bodies did whatever the Party demanded. Gorbachev wanted to trim the power of the Party, and give the government more power to question Party ideas and to act independently.

These ideas came as a breath of fresh air to those in Russia who yearned for a more democratic-style government. Gorbachev became a hero to Western nations. But Yeltsin and Gorbachev began to clash on the fine points of *glasnost* and *perestroika*. For one, Yeltsin began to believe in an idea many old-line Communists found just as shocking—free markets and private property. He eventually decided that a Western-style democracy could not work without a Western economy, where people could operate

businesses and sell goods at a profit. Gorbachev was as
shocked at Yeltsin's ideas as the hardliners were at his own
reforms.

Over time, Yeltsin and Gorbachev fought fierce battles
concerning the Communist ideal of a state-run economy
versus a free market. And despite his commitment to free
speech, Gorbachev often took offense at criticism.
"Gorbachev never seemed comfortable with the new people
created by his own policies—the aggressive liberals who
actually believed in democracy, and acted accordingly,"
wrote an American journalist who lived in Moscow for
years. [3]

Boris Yeltsin was among the most aggressive of those
liberals. He traveled tirelessly, to Moscow's neighborhoods
and to places as distant as icy Siberia. Yeltsin met as many
people as he could, talking to them about their problems,
creating a popular image that many would remember when
they had their historic first chance to vote for their country's
top leader. That day would come sooner than most citizens,
including Yeltsin, then knew.

But first, the republic would have to face up to its chief
problems—the corruption created by seventy years of
inefficient economy and dictatorship. Yeltsin discovered
more about the Soviet Union's dark side during a trip to
Tashkent, a city in the republic of Uzbekistan.

Boris sits with General Secretary Mikhail Gorbachev during the opening of the 1990 Congress of People's Deputies. (AP/Wide World)

When Boris arrived at his hotel, he found himself nearly mobbed by people wanting to see him. The city's officials wanted to seal him off, but Yeltsin would have none of it. He told his bodyguard that over the next few days he would see anyone who wanted to talk with him.

His gesture opened a floodgate. One person after another brought their complaints, appalling stories of bribery and crookedness. The sheer number of such tales overwhelmed him.

Ironically, one of the first visitors was a member of the

KGB, the Soviet Union's feared secret police. The man told Yeltsin that the right amount of money could buy favors from the top leader of the local Uzbek Communist Party. A previous "clean-up" of the party had changed nothing. In essence, party leaders had merely replaced one corrupt secretary with another crook. The new secretary's name was Usmankhodzhaev. The KGB man brought documents to back up his claim. Naturally, Yeltsin's informant could not complain to the very people who had created the web of deceit. Justice could only come from Moscow.

"He was followed by an endless stream of visitors," Yeltsin later wrote. "I listened to what seemed totally improbable but were in fact entirely real stories of bribery in the upper echelons of the Uzbek Communist Party." [4] He resolved to report the corruption he had uncovered to the highest authorities on his return to Moscow.

Before he left, though, he had a run-in with the hotel's managers which he considered yet another example of the rottenness within the system. Perhaps it indicated just as much about his own eccentric ways. When he found his food and lodging expenses had been paid from party funds, Yeltsin exploded in anger. This simple act could have been meant as a bribe. "Unable to restrain myself, almost shouting, I demanded my bill and paid it myself," Yeltsin wrote. [5] His trip was party business, even many honest officials would have found nothing wrong with letting the Party pick up the tab. But Boris had a puritanical streak in his nature that matched his stubbornness.

But Gorbachev was stubborn as well. When Yeltsin returned to Moscow and reported the accusations he had heard in Tashkent, their face-to-face meeting turned into a verbal brawl. The new Uzbek party secretary was not taking bribes, Gorbachev insisted, only trying to clean up the mess left by the rogue he had replaced. As Gorbachev saw it, Usmankhodzhaev was being smeared by the mafia, a criminal organization on which Soviets often blamed corruption. Yeltsin's visitors had fooled him, Gorbachev stated. Yegor Ligachev, the second-highest ranking leader in the Soviet Union, had vouched for the Uzbek secretary. Yeltsin had to bite his tongue. He could not take on the two most powerful men in the Soviet Union in one battle.

The smoke of the latest skirmish had barely cleared when an official phoned to inform Yeltsin that he was to report back to the Politburo at once.

Boris may have expected an official dressing down, but that was far from the case. The system which had rebuked him and raised a stone wall against his warnings was once again ready to boost Yeltsin's power.

SIX

THE PEOPLE'S CHAMPION

The Politburo was the most powerful political body in the Soviet Union. It was composed of the top leaders of the Communist Party, and made the final decisions on almost everything that mattered in the country.

Although the Politburo met regularly, Yeltsin knew this was no routine session as soon as he walked in. There were none of his political peers and no committee chairmen in the room. There were only Mikhail Gorbachev and the other members of the Politburo. For the moment, the powerful body was only concerned with Yeltsin.

Gorbachev wasted no words. He told Yeltsin the Politburo had decided to name him head of the Moscow City Committee, a powerful organization with over a million members. Yeltsin was stunned by the news, and later wondered why Gorbachev had picked him. He decided experience, dedication and toughness must have weighed in his favor.

He was probably right, but Gorbachev also had another reason.

Just as the Politburo had called on Yeltsin's bulldozers to raze the Ipatiev house, it now wanted him to shake the foundations of the Moscow City Committee. Gorbachev needed a human bulldozer, and had decided Yeltsin was his man.

Under Viktor Grishin, former chairman of the city committee, Moscow's public image had suffered because of poor administration. Before the Politburo, Yeltsin proclaimed his reluctance to take on the task of leading such a powerful city committee, and said of Grishin, "The ill effects of his term were manifested in public affairs, the people's standard of living and Moscow's outward appearance." Yeltsin wrote, "Because of him, life in the country's capital was worse than it had been several decades before: dirt, endless lines, overcrowded public transportation."[1]

Gorbachev knew that his rival never took any promotion without first expressing reluctance. It didn't matter in this case, anyway. Gorbachev was determined to have Yeltsin accept the position, and he got it before Yeltsin left the meeting that late December day.

When one clears a forest, chips must fly, as one Soviet leader had said long ago after a bloody purge. In Gorbachev's new age of openness and reform there would be no deadly purges. No one would go to a freezing labor camp, or stand against a wall to face a firing squad. But many a comfortable career would be destroyed, starting with chairman Grishin's.

And when Yeltsin charged into the bureaucratic forest of the Moscow City Committee, chips did fly.

Yeltsin struck the first blow, firing Grishin almost immediately. He did not call it a firing, of course. For the record, Grishin was simply retired and pensioned off, "at his own request", but no party official was fooled.

Yeltsin suspected a counter attack by Grishin's "old guard"at a February meeting of the Moscow party organization, so he headed it off. He made it his business to go over every detail of the city committee's work, interviewing its officials, mapping his way out of the mess Grishin had made. He rolled over his opponents in the February meeting, thundering for two hours about his well-researched goals for Moscow.

"You have brought in a strong and welcome gust of fresh air," Gorbachev said at the end of Yeltsin's speech.[2] But he was not smiling when he said it, Yeltsin noticed. The rift between the two was growing, even as Gorbachev helped his career.

Yeltsin did not hesitate to get rid of bureaucrats. He axed the entire top staff of the City Committee, including Grishin's assistants, then methodically worked his way down through the bureaus, throwing out everyone with any allegiance to the former chairman.

As usual, he did not care who was offended. A high official who had used his position under Grishin to take paid trips all over the world dropped in one day to make a personal pitch for his job. He flattered Yeltsin and downgraded his former boss.

The flattery did not work. Yeltsin bluntly told his new subordinate that he, too, must go. The only concession he made was that the man could retire "decently"—with the usual language about leaving "at his own request." When the official did not deliver his signed resignation to Yeltsin's office the next day as planned, Yeltsin proved he was not joking. He called the reluctant retiree and said that if he did not want go decently, Yeltsin would surely find another way. The resignation landed on his desk in twenty minutes.

Boris had never flinched at being ruthless when he cleared his way in a new job, but he demonstrated compassion for the plight of average workers and quickly established a reputation as a leader who liked to mingle with the people. Yeltsin had become an earnest disciple of Gorbachev's democratic reforms. At the same time, the friction between Yeltsin and Gorbachev grew steadily worse.

Much of the problem between the two men, as Yeltsin saw it, lay in Gorbachev's inner circle, and in the Politburo itself. Many high officials were only too happy to sing the praises of openness and reform, just as they had once spouted the Brezhnev party line, but underneath they were still old-school political hacks. In short, they wanted nothing more from the system than a luxurious lifestyle for themselves.

For a time, Yeltsin enjoyed good favor with the national leadership. They approved of the way he organized raids on lawbreakers, rousted criminals and drug pushers, and attacked corruption in the marketplace. The honeymoon ended, though, when Yeltsin made it clear he considered the extravagant lifestyle of high officials part of the problem.

Many high government leaders preferred to see the city only through the windows of their limousines. Yeltsin's riding on subways and buses, in order to sit shoulder to shoulder with common workers, annoyed other committee chairmen and members of the Politburo. His concern for ordinary people contrasted badly with their unconcern.

Yeltsin denounced Moscow's dirty streets, its overcrowded transportation system and the long lines in the stores. With all the zeal of a newly made reformer, he made a show of walking through the dirt, riding the subways, and standing in lines with people awaiting their meager meat rations.

People talked to Yeltsin more frankly on buses and in the streets than they would have dared in a government office. He saw them before dawn as he rode with them to the factories, rode with them through the subway, and listened to their tired grumbling at the end of the work day. They took him at his word when he asked for candid criticism, and a few did not spare Yeltsin either. People told him he was part of the bureaucracy that had created the mess.

The tough talk did not faze Boris. He found it quite instructive, in fact, and made solutions to the most frequent complaints part of his own agenda. He also promised to change the system. His meet-the-people strategy raised his popularity, while it infuriated high government officials.

Muttered grumblings soon turned to open combat in the Politburo and in the press. Yeltsin lambasted his peers for their isolation from the real world, their insistence on hiding in their limousines and *dachas*. Many party officials, Yeltsin charged, kept their high positions by slavishly following the rules and knowing whom to flatter. He blasted those he considered professional lackeys in an interview with the paper *Moskovskaya Pravda*.

"In recent years, many leaders have outdone even the clergy in ritualism," Yeltsin said. "They know at what point to clap, how to greet the authorities, and what decor to put up for an event. This is the invention of wheeler-dealers and toadies who are trying to keep afloat."[3]

This kind of talk delighted the common people and, of course, further enraged many officials. A newspaper reporter read Yeltsin an anonymous letter, which he said came from the wife of a senior official.

"Don't snipe at us," the woman wrote. "We are the elite, and you cannot halt the stratification of society. You are not strong enough. We will rip up the puny sails of your *perestroika* and you will be unable to reach your destination." [4] Yeltsin made it clear to the interviewer he didn't worry about offending "the elite."

But Yeltsin could not shrug off Gorbachev so easily. Yeltsin's attacks on the leadership eventually forced a public face-off between the two. However, Yeltsin's sense of timing could not have been worse when he chose to level a barrage of criticism toward the elite's Central Committee during a session designed to honor the 70th anniversary of the October Revolution of 1917. It was that revolution which created the Soviet Union, and Gorbachev, who was the principal speaker, naturally wanted a warm reception.

But Boris refused to play by the script. In the customary

critique session after the speech, everyone followed proto-
col and praised Gorbachev's words, until Yeltsin's turn came.
He fired off twenty tough criticisms, most aimed at the party
itself more than at Gorbachev's speech. But Gorbachev's
stare grew cold as Yeltsin's broadside continued, and when
he finished, General Secretary Gorbachev halted the session
and stalked from the room for a break. When Gorbachev
returned, he unleashed a long tirade against Yeltsin. The
furious verbal assault bewildered and stunned Yeltsin in its
intenstiy. "There can be no doubt at that moment Gorbachev
simply hated me," Yeltsin wrote.[5]

Previous criticism had rarely pierced Yeltsin's thick skin
the way Gorbachev's harsh words did. But he did not nurse
his wounds long. Because of Gorbachev's own reforms, he
felt free to counterattack. What good was *perestroika* or
glasnost, he asked, if one had to grovel before their creator?

Yeltsin later admitted the debt he, as well as the rest of
the Soviet Union, owed Gorbachev. The General Secretary
could have taken the luxuries of power, just as his prede-
cessors had, and enjoyed its trappings for the rest of his life.
Instead Gorbachev took the monumental first step toward
making his nation a democracy. "He started by climbing a
mountain whose summit is not even visible," Yeltsin wrote.
"It is somewhere up in the clouds and no one knows how
the ascent will end."[6]

Yeltsin wanted to climb toward democracy as well, and it was on the path up that he would grapple ever more frequently with Gorbachev. Their days as more or less friendly rivals had ended, though Yeltsin's rise had not. He was made a candidate, or non-voting, member of the Politburo on February 18, 1986.

From the time he entered its ranks, Yeltsin became a ticking time bomb in the halls of the Kremlin. Less than two years later, his pent-up fury would explode, and nearly shatter his political career in the process.

Boris rarely went to a session that did not annoy him in some way. He suspected Politburo members, including Gorbachev, liked hearing themselves talk. Many of them were "dunderheads," in Yeltsin's opinion. One of the top dunderheads was Yegor Ligachev, second-highest official in the Communist Party. Ligachev had imposed a series of controls on alcohol which created an underground vodka market, much in the manner of America's Prohibition in the 1920s. Yeltsin blamed Ligachev personally for the thriving black market and the numerous cases of alcohol poisoning resulting from illegally made beverages. Yet the alcohol controls were only one of many issues which eventually caused Yeltsin and Ligachev to despise one another. The fuse finally ignited after a particularly frustrating Politburo session on September 12, 1987. Yeltsin had quarreled furiously that day with Ligachev and returned to his office sick of it all.

Boris sat down at his desk, pulled out a blank sheet of paper and began a letter to Gorbachev. After rambling through a long slate of criticisms aimed at the slow pace of reform, his Politburo enemies and Gorbachev himself, Yeltsin ended with a shocker—he wished to resign both as First Secretary of the Moscow City Committee and as member of the Politburo. He asked Gorbachev's permission to do so.

The letter triggered the painful public spectacle which would become known as "the Yeltsin affair." Boris had put his head in a self-made noose, his peers thought, and then pulled the hangman's lever. And by the time the affair ended, his enemies would be convinced they had seen the last of Boris Yeltsin.

SEVEN

THE
"YELTSIN AFFAIR"

Yeltsin's letter of resignation set off a political firestorm, and, for party leaders, it could not have come at a worse time. With the 70th anniversary of the October Revolution at hand, the Politburo's black sheep threatened to disrupt a solemn celebration. It was almost like a replay of Yeltsin's primary school graduation, when his attack on the hated teacher tarnished the ceremony.

Perhaps hoping to delay the confrontation, Gorbachev at first ignored Yeltsin's resignation letter. He must have had to bite his tongue, considering Yeltsin had made it clear he considered Gorbachev one of the chief obstacles to progress.

"I am personally distressed by the attitude of several of the comrades who make up the membership of the Politburo," Yeltsin wrote. "They are intelligent, and therefore they have quickly become supporters of *perestroika*. But is their conversion sincere? This suits them and, if you will forgive me for saying so, Mikhail Sergeyevich, I believe it also suits you."[1] With this, Yeltsin accused Gorbachev of having created a dynamic where no one close to the General Secretary dared disagree with him.

For a time after he sent the letter, Yeltsin kept what he had done a secret. He told no one, not even his wife Naya. Gorbachev was on holiday at the time. When he returned, he did call Yeltsin, but revealed nothing of his thoughts on the resignation letter. All Gorbachev said about the matter was "Let's meet later," according to Yeltsin.[2]

"Later" stretched to weeks, and Gorbachev still said nothing more about Yeltsin's resignation. Yeltsin decided Gorbachev must have changed his mind, and planned to put the matter of his resignation before the Central Committee. Yeltsin made his own preparations for the assembly of the Central Committee, where he would deliver what could well be his last address. And characteristically he would not go quietly.

As noted, Boris' attack was badly timed. Yeltsin's effort to expose the corrupt system was also a one-man war. He had made no effort to round up any allies to support him. He risked looking like a crazy man, a person with many enemies and no friends. And Yeltsin's hard-driving style may have finally caught up with him, affecting his judgement. He was nearing exhaustion. The factory visits, the bus rides, the long arguments in the Politburo left him no free time. He had been working 18-hour days, maintaining a pace set in his youth. But in Moscow, his addiction to work had taken its toll. Yeltsin would come home and just sit in his car for half an hour at a time, too tired to move.

Whatever the cause of Boris' impatience, he did not wait for the polite moment to voice his anger. He launched an attack on Gorbachev on Oct 21, 1987, during the Politburo planning meeting for the 70th anniversary of the October Revolution.

Gorbachev spoke first, then opened the floor for criticism. All he heard was praise—until Yeltsin spoke. Boris went to the podium with no notes, and to the shock of other Politburo members began attacking every statement in Gorbachev's speech.

Most omniously for Gorbachev, Yeltsin said, "Recently there has been a noticeable increase in what I can only call adulation of the general secretary by certain full members of the Politburo," Yeltsin said, and later added "This tendency to adulation is absolutely unacceptable. To criticize to people's faces—yes, that is necessary—but not to develop a taste for adulation, which can become the norm again, which can become a 'cult of personality.'"[3]

No one in Yeltsin's highly uncomfortable audience could have missed the meaning of the expression "cult of personality". He was describing Gorbachev in the same terms others had used to describe the brutal dictator Joseph Stalin.

Boris ended with much the same words he had used to close his resignation letter. Yeltsin would resign from the Politburo. He would turn over the chairmanship of his Moscow committee into the hands of the Central Committee.

Yeltsin's overworked heart hammered in his chest as he sat down. Later, he would ponder why he did not choose to wait for a better time to unleash his onslaught of criticisms. "I often wondered afterward whether I might have chosen a different approach," he wrote, "whether I really needed to have charged in as I did, guns blazing; to have caused the uproar that resulted in such a drastic change in my life."[4]

For the moment, at least, he felt he had done the right thing. He certainly achieved one of his objectives. He had badly shaken the complacency of the Politburo. And as he well knew, he would stand as the lightning rod in the political storm that followed.

Stinging rebukes were hurled at him from the podium. Old friends joined Yeltsin's worst foes in accusing him of cowardice, hypocrisy, lying and political incorrectness. In so doing, they proved Yeltsin right on one count—old-school Soviet tactics were alive and well in the age of *perestroika* and *glasnost*. The ritual humiliation of Yeltsin looked and sounded like a scene from the Communist past.

When the verbal barrage finally ended, Gorbachev gave Yeltsin his chance to reply. Like a fighter on the ropes, Yeltsin did not attack, but only defended, and even retreated a few steps. He said he had not intended to divide the party leadership. He took back part of his criticism about Gorbachev's "cult of personality;" Yeltsin said he was referring only to a few over-enthusiastic admirers, not all Politburo members. But Gorbachev was not appeased. "You know what the cult of personality is . . . Are you so politically illiterate we have to organize a class here to teach you how to read and write?" Someone shouted from the floor, accusing Yeltsin of trying to further his ambition. "I think so, too," Gorbachev said. "Isn't it enough that all Moscow revolves around your person? Do you need the Central Committee to bother itself about you as well?" Gorbachev then demanded Yeltsin's reply.[5]

Boris knew he was defeated. "Apart from some expressions, I am as a whole in agreement," he said. "By letting down the Central Committee and the Moscow city organization in my speech today, I made a mistake."[6]

Then Gorbachev revealed for the first time to the Polit-buro that he had received a resignation letter from Yeltsin. And then he proposed that the Central Committee rule Yeltsin's speech mistaken, but leave him on the Politburo for the time being. After the anniversary, Gorbachev would ask for the Moscow party to replace Yeltsin as first secretary. Gorbachev hoped this compromise would keep the news of the conflict between the two leaders out of the press.

Reports quickly began to surface in the stories of foreign correspondents, who soon began clamoring for an answer to a simple question: Had Yeltsin resigned or not? A Central Committee member released the bare details of the cantan-kerous meeting. Meanwhile, Yeltsin carried on his duties as usual.

Boris received some support from a few unexpected sources. During the Revolution Day ceremonies, while Boris walked in procession with other national leaders toward Lenin's Tomb on Red Square, two world leaders went out of their way to encourage him. Cuban dictator Fidel Castro went beyond the ritual of shaking hands by embrac-ing Yeltsin three times in Russian tradition. Then he said something in Spanish that Boris could not understand, but nonetheless sounded sympathetic in tone. Yeltsin had taken only a few additional steps when Polish leader Wojciech

Jaruzelski also embraced him. As Gorbachev looked on, Jaruzelski said "Stand firm, Boris Nikolayevich!"[7]

The sympathetic words did help lighten Yeltsin's depression. Yet stress, exhaustion, and physical neglect collected their toll. Two days later, Yeltsin collapsed and had to be taken to a hospital. Doctors fed Yeltsin tranquilizers and other medicines, stuck needles and tubes into his arms, and forbade him to leave his bed. Agonizing headaches racked his skull in the early morning hours, and doctors deemed him so ill they would not even let his wife Naya in to see him. Boris Yeltsin's later writings imply the illness which sent him to the hospital was severe tension and exhaustion. Other writers say he suffered a heart attack. Whatever the case, he spent much of his time in the hospital in a drug-induced stupor.

Imagine then the patient's surprise, when on the morning of November 11, 1987, he got a call from Gorbachev. The General Secretary wanted to see Yeltsin right away. "You must come and see me for a short time, Boris Nikolayevich," Gorbachev said. "After that, perhaps we will go and attend the plenum of the Moscow City Committee together."[8]

Yeltsin protested he could not possibly leave the hospital; his physicians had forbidden it. But the doctors proved flexible when confronted by higher authority. They pumped him full of sedatives and painkillers, as the KGB agents guarding Yeltsin prepared to take him before Gorbechev and his committee.

Naya flew into a rage when she found out. She begged Boris not to go, then turned her anger on the head officer of the KGB. She called the order to pull Yeltsin from his hospital bed an act of sadism, and demanded that the agents do their duty and protect her husband. In his condition, she protested they could be dragging him to his death. But the KGB, which had in the past dragged many a healthy citizen to his or her death, obeyed its orders.

Yeltsin could barely walk when he was escorted into the meeting of the City Committee. What followed seemed like a waking nightmare, intensified by Yeltsin's pain and the haze of the drugs. He had been summoned to be fired from office in a cruel ritual.

Again he was attacked with angry speeches. Gorbachev began by calling Yeltsin's October 21 speech immature and self-contradictory. Yeltsin's commitment to reform was only a political act, Gorbachev charged.

One official said Yeltsin had encouraged trouble, because he thought he looked his best in a fight. Another repeated the criticism that Yeltsin had ridden subways and met with common people only to enhance his own glory. A man who had worked for Yeltsin said he bullied his workers and made their lives miserable. The verbal thrashing went on for more than four hours.

Throughout this torment, Yeltsin held his head in his hands. A journalist recalled that Yeltsin's face looked blue, his lips purple. His enemy Ligachev sat beside him, gloating in triumph.[9]

Then came Yeltsin's turn to defend himself. He staggered to the front of the room, and in the style of the Stalin era, obediently confessed his sins. Yet his words could barely be understood, as he struggled against the effects of the drugs and exhaustion. Yes, he said, all his words in October had been false, the imaginings of an overworked mind, driven only by ambition. He apologized personally to Gorbachev, and admitted a "great burden of guilt."

It was then the shame of the event finally seemed to pierce the armor of Gorbachev's anger. He watched Yeltsin's "confession" with visible discomfort, shaking his head as a blush rose in his cheeks. It was if he realized he had gone too far, just as he had accused Yeltsin of doing.

When the meeting broke up, Boris remained slumped in his seat as if paralyzed, again with head in hands. Gorbachev started to leave, looked back at his vanquished rival, then went to his side. He helped Yeltsin to his feet, and they walked down the hall together to wait in Yeltsin's office until an ambulance arrived to take Yeltsin back to the hospital.[10]

A few days later, Gorbachev again called Boris in the hospital. Springing yet another surprise, he offered Yeltsin a new government job—First Deputy Chairman of the State Committee for Construction. Yeltsin accepted. Perhaps Gorbachev felt some pain and embarrassment for the inquisition by the city committee. Or perhaps, as Yeltsin later speculated, Gorbachev needed his "bad boy," just to show that under his reformed government, even dissenters could hold a place. Anyone who had witnessed the sorry spectacle of November 11 might have doubted that notion, however.

Boris Yeltsin's career seemed to be at an end. But if he had drawn the noose, his efforts may have also helped snap the rope. One of the orders he gave while Moscow City Chairman had been that proceedings like those of the November 11 City Committee meeting would be published in Pravda. Yet the government repressed the text of Yeltsin's resignation speech, and people began to wonder why. What did the supposedly new and open regime have to fear? The public demanded to read about the proceedings.

Yeltsin's accusers, even Gorbachev, may have underestimated the public's new attention to political matters. It was the ultimate triumph of Gorbachev's, and at the same time, a hidden trap for his anti-Yeltsin strategy. As events of the following months proved, the Yeltsin affair had not ended.

Gorbachev and Yeltsin would learn a lesson together: Once the genie of democracy is unleashed, it is no easy task to send it back into the bottle.

EIGHT

TRIUMPH IN EXILE

"I looked inside and there was no one there," Yeltsin wrote about himself after his humiliation before the committee.[1] When released from the hospital, Yeltsin dutifully reported for the deputy chairman's job at the Gosstroi construction department. But his inner fire had gone out.

Much of the public had not liked what it saw of the Yeltsin affair. Letters poured into the newspapers and the Central Committee, either supporting Yeltsin or asking uncomfortable questions of the establishment. The attack on Yeltsin also did not go unnoticed in his home province of Sverdlovsk. People protested, and the local post office had so many pro-Yeltsin letters they put up a sign saying that no mail addressed to Boris in Moscow would be accepted.[2] Moscow citizens, too, began to wonder if Yeltsin had become a martyr.

Public sympathy was not enough to lift Yeltsin from exile. His status allowed him to continue attending plenary sessions of the Central Committee, but encounters with old colleagues created mutual discomfort.

Yeltsin thought his new job tedious at first, an outpost in limbo. Depression and ill health followed him home at night. He sometimes suffered until dawn with blinding headaches. His wife and daughters had to summon emergency medical crews. When Naya and his daughters, Lena and Tanya, attempted to comfort him, they frequently suffered his irrational anger. The three women had always struggled to make the Yeltsin home an island of tranquility, where Boris could escape after his bruising political battles. He loved them for the tenderness they brought to his life, and later referred to them as "the women's great council," for they made most family decisions. Yet Boris did not always repay their kindness during his time of political exile. He sometimes vented his anger on his devoted family, though his outbursts at Naya and his daughters later left him feeling embarrassed and ashamed.

Naya exercised self-control, and refrained from talking about political topics during family time. But Boris' fits after his expulsion from the Politburo surely wore her nerves raw at times. "In general, it's hard to be a wife," Boris later admitted. "Being my wife is even harder."[3]

Boris, accompanied by his wife Naya, waves to supporters during his 1990 campaign for President of the Russian Republic. (AP/Wide World)

Perhaps Boris' family realized his struggle against depression marked a struggle for his life—and not just his political life. Rumors circulated that he had considered suicide. He thrashed in his sleep as he dreamed of the committee inquisition.

The few doctors he trusted gave him advice similar to that for a patient in grief—wait, and let time do its work. Yeltsin's body had survived the brink of collapse. His energy and mood would rise as the painful memories receded.

Time proved them right. Boris gradually began to heal. He describes his entire time in the construction chairman's job as nightmarish, but even his account lists some bright spots. He took pride in the realization that his knowledge of the industry remained sharp, despite changes since his last construction management job. He analyzed what powers his new position left him, and began to use them. Yeltsin still kept his workaholic habits, but paced himself better.

In his encounters with people in the street, Boris began to see the possibility of his political rebirth. Average citizens bolstered his recovery by greeting him fondly and saying that they agreed with his ideas and admired his courage. He realized anew the benefits of being a black sheep in an increasingly unpopular regime.

At first, the politicians who had battered and dismissed him did not realize they were helping to make Yeltsin a popular hero. Reporters for Soviet state-run papers tried to slip Yeltsin stories past their editors, and foreign journalists sought him out.

The elections for the Nineteenth Party Congress in 1988 provided Boris a re-entry into politics. He decided to be a candidate. To do this, he would have to survive every trick his enemies in the Party could throw at him to earn the nomination. As the elections approached, grassroots groups tried to nominate him, but Party officials worked to disqualify him. Finally, he earned delegate status at the last minute during an assembly in the small republic of Karelia. Yeltsin could not have chosen a more charged forum for his comeback. The Nineteenth Party Congress would be the first since the 1920s to allow dissenting opinions, and the first ever to be shown on television. In the 1980s, Soviet politicians would learn what American office seekers had known for years: making a good impression on television is critical.

Although other delegates crowded around for a glimpse of Yeltsin, temporarily sacrificing their official dignity for a look at this notorious rebel, those who ran the convention almost succeeded in blocking Yeltsin's speech. They kept him muzzled until the fifth and final day. But then Yeltsin broke the leash in his characteristic way. He and the Karelian delegation stormed the rostrum.

The organizers had squeezed Yeltsin's group into the highest reaches of the balcony. As the Karelian delegation began to march down the aisle, people stopped listening to the speaker to watch the unannounced march. By the time the Karelian group charged to the middle of the auditorium, all eyes were turned toward them.

Panic erupted among some of the loyal Communist deputies who were determined to maintain order. Assistants to the Central Committee tried a number of ploys to force

Yeltsin to withdraw and return to his seat, but finally he won the rostrum through sheer stubbornness.

If Yeltsin's foes had hoped he would repeat his self-destructive behavior of the 1987 plenum, they were disappointed. Yeltsin strongly defended his criticisms of the system. He looked like a new man, and his rebirth happened before the entire nation, as the television cameras transmitted the image of an unbowed warrior facing down powerful enemies.

Yeltsin blasted party officials for isolating themselves from criticism, *perestroika's* architects for failing to achieve their mission, the Communist Party for burying its head in the sand and pretending all was well. Yeltsin challenged the Soviet custom—purging or exiling its leaders when they became politically inconvenient, then "rehabilitating" or making heroes of them after they were dead. Shouts broke out, followed by a call for order.

"Comrade delegates!" Yeltsin said. "I am asking for my personal political rehabilitation, while I am still alive."[4] Yeltsin left the podium, having had the last word of the morning session.

Finding himself faced with a fresh challenge from this rival who would not die, Gorbachev was forced to wait until after the lunch break before allowing speeches in reply. One of the first to speak was Yeltsin's old foe Yegor Ligachev. He criticized Yeltsin for food shortages during his administration of the Sverdlovsk province. If he had let it go at that, Ligachev might have scored a point. Instead, he raised again a tired accusation that Yeltsin had already answered—his alleged preference for interviews with foreign journalists. It was a blatant attempt to accuse Yeltsin of being too friendly with the Soviet Union's enemies.

"Do you like having all the foreigners running around you, Boris?" Ligachev chided.[5]

The insult stunned television viewers. In official meetings, Russian etiquette requires that people address one another by both their first and middle names. Ligachev should have called Yeltsin "Boris Nikolayevich." But he chose to talk to Yeltsin in the manner one addresses children. If the meeting had gone on behind closed doors, as before, Ligachev's crude insult would have been recorded only in party records. Instead, it echoed across the nation. In the weeks and months that followed, newspaper writers, speakers and cartoonists lambasted Ligachev for his rudeness. Gorbachev answered Yeltsin's criticisms later in the session, but his rebuttal contained one damning omission—he failed to utter a word in Ligachev's defense.

Three months later, Gorbachev's deeds admitted the

truth of many of Yeltsin's criticisms. He swept through the ranks of the party apparatus, firing, retiring and demoting many among the old guard. Ligachev, for instance, was dropped from number two man in the party. Gorbachev never mentioned Yeltsin's name when he made the changes, but Yeltsin's words to the nation had clearly made reorganization necessary.

Boris' televised fight with Ligachev helped complete his spectacular rise from outcast to folk hero. Students at a Communist Party school, the Higher Komsomol Group, won a battle with the school leader to let Yeltsin speak at one of their meetings. Yeltsin was a hit with the students, speaking candidly for five hours about his scandal and the shortcomings of Gorbachev's programs. People wrote him letters, and walked up to him in the street to shake his hand and praise his courage. When he went to Moscow's Bolshoi Theater, the audience immediately recognized him and spontaneous applause broke out in the hall.

In late 1988, the Supreme Soviet, once the tool of dictators, approved a historic step toward democracy. It voted to allow elections to be held for the Congress of People's Deputies in March of the following year. These would be the first free elections in the USSR in seventy years. The Supreme Soviet had opened the gates for Yeltsin's triumphant return.

Boris filed for the office of at-large deputy from Moscow, the nation's largest electoral district. Playing a role he had mastered, Yeltsin cast himself as a man fighting for the people against a powerful, arrogant and pampered leadership. He called for popular votes on important issues, an end to the luxuries enjoyed by high officials, and for the Communist Party to follow the wishes of the new Congress of People's Deputies instead of dictating to it. When Yeltsin supporters rallied in Gorky Park, the Party tried an old tactic—police suppression. But instead of dispersing, the crowd grew larger. The mob charged city hall, carrying signs reading HANDS OFF YELTSIN![6]

In the end, Yeltsin triggered an electoral landslide that crushed the Party. He won five million votes—more than 89% of the total. Moreover, he helped spark a popular rebellion. Throughout the country, old-line party bosses were toppled in their first brush with democracy.

In a way, Gorbachev had gotten what he wanted when the old Party hacks were defeated, although most observers considered the elections a rebuke of his policies. Some analysts said Gorbachev got more *perestroika* than he had bargained for. The people had cast their votes against "business as usual" and had discovered a new and thrilling sense of power. And there appeared to be no road back to the old ways of dictatorship and repression.

Yeltsin had won both vindication and a new office. Another may have rested on his laurels after such a victory, but not Yeltsin. His stunning triumph in the elections of 1989 rekindled the old fire of ambition in his heart.

NINE

PRESIDENT YELTSIN

Mikhail Gorbachev had looked into the future of the Soviet Union and had seen the need for change. But his vision failed him when he tried to see into the mind of Boris Yeltsin. This failure was made clear when, about a week before the opening session of the new Congress, he called on his old adversary.

The meeting did not go well. It marked the first time the two had seen each other in person for some time, and both men felt uncomfortable. Yeltsin still blamed Gorbachev for trying to banish him into political exile. Gorbachev still bore scars from his rejection by the voters. Furthermore, Yeltsin's triumph at the election booth had rubbed salt into his wounds.

Gorbachev's principal concern was how Yeltsin intended to use his new office. Gorbachev's main fear was that Yeltsin would try to do too much too fast, and wreck Gorbachev's reforms. In turn, Yeltsin wanted to know how dedicated Gorbachev was to true democratic reform—helping the people, in Yeltsin's words—and how much for saving "the system that had brought the country to the brink of disaster."[1]

In truth, Gorbachev was dedicated to both. Many analysts have come to believe that Gorbachev's main weakness as a leader was that he never clearly defined his goals: he wanted both to preserve the Soviet system and to change it. These conflicting goals are what led to his failure.

The meeting was not a success. Neither man's position was compatible with the other. "His answers were brusque and harsh, and the longer we talked, the thicker grew the wall between us," Yeltsin wrote.[2] Gorbachev even tried to offer Yeltsin a ministerial job, if he would give up his elected position. Yeltsin wasted no time in rejecting Gorbachev's proposal. The meeting ended after an hour and accomplished nothing. Yeltsin had made his break with the old Soviet system. He knew his future rested firmly in the hands of the Russian people.

Gorbachev also desperately desired for all the peoples of the Soviet Union to trust him. Although he had lost ground in the election, he wanted the new Congress to succeed. He still believed in the principle of *glasnost*. And in that spirit, he decided the entire session of Congress would be televised. Even Yeltsin had to give Gorbachev credit for this bold decision: "Those ten days, in which almost the whole country watched the desperate debates of the Congress, unable to tear themselves away from their television sets, gave the people more of a political education than seventy years of stereotyped Marxist-Leninist lectures multiplied a millionfold and flung at the Soviet people in order to turn them into dummies," Yeltsin wrote later.[3]

The first drama developed quickly. The law which had set up the Congress created a free-for-all in the races for seats in the upper body of the Congress, the Supreme Soviet. Having taken nearly 90% of the vote in his race, Yeltsin expected a seat on the Supreme Soviet. Ironically, Gorbachev also wanted Yeltsin on the Supreme Soviet. He did not want this new Congress to look like a rubber stamp.

Trouble came from some of Gorbachev's more conservative allies—those Yeltsin called the "silent and obedient majority."[4] Many of the conservatives, sometimes referred to as hardliners, did not support Gorbachev's reforms. They longed for the days of Stalin and Brezhnev. But they realized that in the current political environment, Gorbachev was the best they could hope for, so they reluctantly supported him.

These conservatives, however, saw Yeltsin as their chief enemy, and blocked his path to the Supreme Soviet.

Anger erupted on the floor when Yeltsin failed to win election to the upper chamber. One delegate complained that the Congress had elected a Supreme Soviet which looked like a body formed by Joseph Stalin or Leonid Brezhnev. Yeltsin was patient, knowing his popularity would force a solution. It was Gorbachev who sweated—without Yeltsin in the Supreme Soviet no one would take its actions seriously. Finally, one delegate already elected to the Supreme Soviet solved the crisis. Alexei Kazannik, a bearded college professor, said he would resign his Supreme Soviet seat on the condition it went to Yeltsin.

"Tell me, Boris Nikolayevich, what will I tell my constituents?" Kazannik said. "For they know the six million people of Moscow are behind you. If I remain, they will kill me."[5] Yeltsin accepted the offer.

Russia's first live televised political drama electrified Russian viewers. And Yeltsin had what it took to make "good television"—a booming voice, ramrod posture, a mane of silver-gray hair and a reputation as a rebel. After his fights on the floor of the Congress, people mobbed Yeltsin in the streets, wanting to touch him, wanting him to kiss their babies. The public could not get enough of this man who had been thought politically dead less than two years before.

Yeltsin used his power cleverly most of the time, but sometimes mishandled his new-found fame. He used the clout he had gained to quickly form a radical group which reflected his vision of *perestroika*. It was called the Inter-Regional Group of Deputies (IRGD). The group preached, among other things, that people should be allowed to own private land. Yeltsin was beginning to publicly speak of his lack of faith in Communism. The formation of the IRGD group widened the gap between Yeltsin and Gorbachev, who adamantly opposed the concept of privately-owned property.

But Yeltsin's fame had begun to overshadow his beliefs. While the radical ideas of the IGRD infuriated hardline communists, alleged scandals during his first trip to America fascinated the Russian public far more.

By now something of a world celebrity, Boris looked forward to his trip to America. When his plane circled the Statue of Liberty, Yeltsin applauded in delight. While visiting a New York fruit and vegetable store, he admitted his Communist teachers had given him a distorted viewpoint of America. "It appears that capitalism is not rotting away, as we were told, but seems to be prospering," he said. "The Statue of Liberty is not some sort of a witch, but a very attractive lady."[6]

He could not believe his eyes when he saw American

supermarkets. "When I saw those shelves crammed with hundreds, thousands of cans, cartons, and goods of every possible sort, for the first time I felt quite frankly sick with despair for the Soviet people," he wrote.[7]

President George Bush handled Yeltsin carefully. He knew a wrong move could offend Gorbachev. Bush's National Security advisor, Brent Scowcroft, called Yeltsin from Baltimore to arrange a meeting in Washington. The meeting lasted two hours, and the President joined the other men for about fifteen minutes. Bush wanted to allow Yeltsin to say he had met the American president, but not formally in the White House. It was an attempt to avoid snubbing Yeltsin without appearing to embrace him.

Despite the deliberately cool reception he received from the Bush administration, Yeltsin's spirits remained high. He enjoyed meeting people in the streets of New York, Washington and Houston as much as he had in Moscow. He showered his hosts with heartfelt praise in his speeches. To an audience in Miami he said, "Although I am not a religious believer, I sometimes have a dream about heaven when I am asleep, and what I saw of Miami, by helicopter yesterday and today by car, was something that far exceeded any vision of paradise that I might have ever had in any dream."[8]

Yeltsin did not know, however, that there were traps in this heaven. One of them was the American press, which

During a visit to the United States in 1989, Boris expresses surprise at the ample supplies of food in a Houston, Texas grocery store. (AP/Wide World)

held the power to make a buffoon of its subjects. The lights of the television cameras flashed on, and reporter's micro-recorders whirred every time Yeltsin stepped off a plane, into a corridor, or into a room where he was to deliver a speech. Experienced American politicians knew how to avoid mis-steps, but Yeltsin blundered into several public relations fiascos like a bear into a steel trap.

First, his drinking got him into trouble. One reporter wrote that Yeltsin had drunk a bottle and a half of Jack Daniel's bourbon in one night in Boston. Whether or not the story was true, it set Yeltsin up for increasingly unflattering portraits in print. Yeltsin tripped up again at a breakfast speech at Johns Hopkins University in Baltimore. Although Yeltsin's aides contradict the story, reporters described Yeltsin as hungover or still drunk at the breakfast speech, staggering and slurring his words and almost falling at one point. Yeltsin's aides later said he was not in the best of shape because he had been unable to sleep until 4 a.m. the night before, and took a sedative which impaired his coordination and speech. When the newspapers came out, describing Yeltsin as a grotesque, though sometimes colorful drunk, his aides were so shocked they hid the papers.

Yeltsin was therefore puzzled when he visited a hog farm outside Indianapolis and the owner casually mentioned his drinking. Inviting Yeltsin into his house, the farmer said

"Unfortunately, I don't have any of your favorite, Jack Daniels."Yeltsin did not understand. When he got back into his car, Yeltsin turned to one of his handlers. "Lev, I did not quite hear it. Which Jack was he talking about?"[9]

By the time a weary Yeltsin returned home, the Russian papers were treating the trip as the misadventures of a country bumpkin in a strange land. Soviet television, still under the control of the Communists, ran a documentary about the trip, one which Yeltsin swore used doctored film to make his speech appear more slurred than it actually had been. A story which appeared in *Pravda*, the official government paper, claimed that Yeltsin had spent his lecture fees loading himself up with souvenirs, clothes and video cassette tapes from American stores. In fact, Yeltsin had used the fees to buy one million disposable hypodermic needles to combat AIDS in Russia.

A fury, dark even by Boris' standards, seized him. The journalist who had written the story about Yeltsin's tourist-style spending retracted it and apologized, as did *Pravda*. However, that was not enough for Yeltsin. He threatened to thrash the paper's editor at a Central Committee meeting. "But I would knock you down, and lying there on the floor would be a piece of something, and the members of the Central Committee would have to look at that piece of something," Yeltsin angrily told the editor. "I despise you.

Sometimes I am sorry that the age of duels is over."[10]

Boris's image problem grew worse when he contracted pneumonia after running his car into the Moscow river. Versions of the incident vary to this day. Yeltsin at first said his automobile had been run off the bridge by his political opponents. His detractors tried to make it look suspiciously like another incident of drunkenness. Yeltsin later retracted his story of being forced off the road. But he never clarified the matter. Instead, he dismissed it as his "private life," and despite initial uproar the story eventually died.

Yeltsin's enormous popularity helped him weather these embarrassments. After the newspapers savaged him for his alleged antics in America, telegrams of sympathy poured in from all across Russia. One high-ranking member of Gorbachev's inner circle explained it this way: "The reaction of the man in the street [to reports of Yeltsin's drinking] was 'So what? He's one of us.' All these things actually help Yeltsin be more popular."[11]

The continued wave of support did more than soothe Boris's ego; it prepared him for the next step in his rise to power. The Congress, largely at Yeltsin's urging, was moving closer to demanding that an election be held for the new office of President of Russia. Yeltsin, and everyone else, knew he would make a powerful candidate.

Boris was elected president of the Russian Congress in

May of 1990, and so became chairman of the Russian Supreme Soviet. But he looked forward to a popular election that would give him more clout than Gorbachev. Gorbechev, who had been elected president of the Soviet Union by the Soviet Congress of People's Deputies, had never stood for election by the nation as a whole, and his popularity was declining.

Boris seized upon this weakness of Gorbachev's. It might be said that Yeltsin's advantage over all his opponents, in the long run, was a deeper respect for the will of the people. After his election as head of the Congress, he knew that maintaining his allegiance to the Communist Party was incompatible with his faith in democracy. In July of 1990, Boris stunned the nation by resigning from the Communist Party.

The stage was set for a showdown over the Russian presidency. The people would choose their president on June 12, 1991.

From the beginning, Yeltsin was the overwhelming favorite. But to avoid the complications of a runoff, he needed to win by at least a 50% majority. His strongest rival was Nikolai Ryzhkov, the former prime minister. Gorbachev had picked a candidate, Vadim Bakatin, to run for the office as well. Vadim Bakatin was a liberal interior minister whom Gorbachev had once fired under pressure from conservatives. Albert Makashov, a general who had made his reputation with a widely publicized attack on Gorbachev's foreign policies in 1990, also posed something of a threat to Boris.

One other candidate, Vladimir Zhirinovsky, received less attention. But Zhirinovsky would soon make a name for himself as a spokesman for the farthest fringe of Russian right-wing politics, the faction which wanted the government to function as a dictatorship.

Boris used an American-style tactic in his choice of a running mate. Most Russians saw Yeltsin as a radical, so he chose a conservative as a running mate—Alexander Rutskoi, an air force pilot who had earned military honors in the Afghan war. Rutskoi had graying hair, a huge mustache, and great charisma among crowds. However, Rutskoi was still a member of the Communist Party. Later, this political difference between Yeltsin and his vice-president would result in bloodshed.

He later admitted that he picked Rutskoi for the wrong reasons: because of his attractive appearance, and because he was a hero of the ill-fated Soviet war in Afghanistan. "Middle-aged matrons would swoon with delight at the sight of such a vice president," is how Boris described why he picked Rutskoi.[12] Rutskoi turned out to be as vain and ambitious as the matinee idol he so resembled. Boris would soon pay a heavy price for not making a wiser choice.

But the conflict with his vice-president was two years in the future. During the early summer of 1991, Boris tangled for the first time with the racist and ultra-nationalist rantings of Zhirinovsky. Although Yeltsin's high support in the opinion polls did not force him to take Zhirinovsky seriously, the public perceived the two as the most colorful contestants in an otherwise boring slate of candidates. Zhirinovsky, at the time perceived as a bizarre extremist, gave the people a chilling look at the threat he would later take to the international stage. How would Zhirinovsky feed a huge country like Russia, someone asked. "Very simply," he said. "I'll move the troops, about 1.5 million strong, into the former East Germany, rattle my nuclear sabers, and they'll give me everything. What price Paris? How about London? Washington? Los Angeles? How much are you willing to pay so I don't wipe them from the face of the earth with my SS-18s? You doubt me. Want to take a chance? Let's get started."[13]

Zhirinovsky rattled off similar threats at almost every major country in the world, with the specter of nuclear attack in nearly every speech. His goal, he said, was to restore the Russian empire to its former glory.

Boris kept his distance from such extremism, while refuting Zhirinovsky's dark threats and claims of ultra-patriotism. "It has become perfectly clear that patriotism lies not only in words about the love of the Russian past, not only in empty admiration of the uniqueness of our national character, and not only in fencing ourselves off from the rest of humanity," Yeltsin said.[14]

Despite Zhirinovsky's ravings, the election year of 1991 belonged to Yeltsin. Everywhere he was met with cheering crowds, pro-Yeltsin signs, and even love notes passed from women during question-and-answer sessions. He protested that his popularity did not come from his having been "trained in Hollywood," but the results of the election could have been written by a movie scripwriter. Boris crushed all his opponents in a landslide, collecting 57.4% of the vote. Ryzhkov came in second. Zhirinovsky surprised—and frightened—his critics by coming in an unexpected third.

Almost overnight the balance of power changed in Russia, especially for Mikhail Gorbachev, who had never faced a popular election. Yeltsin, by contrast, now held an office elected by the people.

In the flush of victory, Boris returned for another visit to America. Deftly avoiding his prior mistakes, he erased the image of the blundering Russian bear. He met with President Bush, this time officially at the White House. Again, he thrilled the crowds. When an admirer gave him a cowboy hat on Capitol Hill, he put it on without hesitation.

He cheerfully charged into a crowd of tourists at the Lincoln Memorial. The shouts that rang up echoed those he had heard in his Russian campaign—"Boris, Boris!"[15]

While Yeltsin enjoyed the afterglow of his victory and Gorbachev labored to patch up his shaky political machine, a new threat developed.

Perhaps Gorbachev should have sensed the peril earlier. He may have been slow to focus on the danger coming from inside his own cabinet because of his concern about Yeltsin and the more liberal reformers.

Over the preceding months, as Yeltsin and his supporters had posed a threat, Gorbachev had turned increasingly to the conservative, old-style Communists for support. By the summer of 1991, Gorbachev found himself in the paradoxical position of depending upon the enemies of reform in order to get his reforms enacted. Clearly, it was an impossible position.

In June, four conservative ministers banded together in a "constitutional coup"—an attempt to topple Gorbachev by legal means. They proposed that Gorbachev turn over his most important powers to Prime Minister Valentin Pavlov. Gorbachev won the battle in Congress, but he did not seek to get rid of his disloyal colleagues. He had no one else to turn to. The hardliners remained in his inner circle, like well-camouflaged snakes waiting to strike.

The hardliners were finally emboldened to attempt an unconstitutional coup because of the negotiations over the proposed Union Treaty. The Soviet Union was actually a huge empire of various republics. Some of the republics had been part of a greater Russia for a long time; others had been forced into the Soviet Union by Stalin's tanks. Over the years, many of the republics had made clear their desire to be free of Moscow's control.

The Union Treaty had grown out of a series of meetings between Gorbachev and the leaders of the various republics held in Novo-Ogaryovo, a suburb of Moscow, over the first months of 1991. Yeltsin had attended the meetings, although he had not then been elected president of Russia. He joined the leaders of the other republics in arguing for more freedom from Moscow. They also insisted on a new constitution that would give them more control over their economies. Gorbachev had originally resisted the idea of loosening Soviet control. As he slowly realized the hardliners would never truly support his reforms, he turned to the men at the Novo-Ogaryovo meeting and told them he would sign a new Union Treaty. Although the agreement would not totally dissolve the Soviet Union, it would go a great way toward ending the central control that Stalin and later Soviet leaders had worked so hard to develop.

While Gorbachev hoped that the new treaty would gain support for his economic and political reforms, both he and Yeltsin knew the Union Treaty was politically explosive. The conservatives denounced the treaty as being the end of the Soviet Union, and publicly stated they would not stand idly by and watch the USSR vanish.

Although he and the General Secretary were long-time enemies, Yeltsin was willing to support Gorbachev when he took such a bold step. Boris was quite aware of the potential for danger the Union Treaty created. During a meeting held to make plans for the formal signing of the treaty, that was to occur in August 20 of 1991, Boris insisted that he and Gorbachev step out onto a balcony to finish their discussion. Boris was convinced they were being bugged. Gorbachev protested, and thought Yeltsin was being overly dramatic.[16] But time would soon reveal that Boris was right. Less than a month after their conversation on the balcony, both Yeltsin and Gorbachev would face an upheaval that would change their lives, and the Soviet Union, forever.

TEN

THE

AUGUST COUP

On the morning of August 19th, 1991, Moscow citizens heard an urgent bulletin from the TASS government news agency. In the beginning, some people thought the story a hoax.

Mikhail Gorbachev had lost his presidency, the broadcast proclaimed. He could no longer perform his job because his health had failed him. All presidential power would immediately be assumed by the Soviet Vice-President, Gennady Yanayev, who would rule with the assistance of a new, mysterious group called the Emergency Committee.

Immediately after this first announcement came another more frightening one: the Committee had decided to shut down the machinery of democracy. It ordered newspapers to cease publication, proclaimed power over television broadcasts, and banned public demonstrations. Moscow Radio attempted to take the sting out of the bizarre announcements by playing soothing classical music, most Muscovites suspected the truth. The Emergency Committee was attempting to kill democracy. A sort of emotional paralysis seized the city, and the workers who reported to their jobs seemed numb.

"Even though democracy was only a baby," TASS reporter Alexander Merkushev, wrote later, "we had somehow gotten used to its durability, and the announcements by the Emergency Committee seemed surreal, totally out of this world."[1] But the nightmare was real. The Emergency Committee, a group of hardline Communists, had staged a coup, or political take-over, of the Soviet Union.

Boris's Yeltsin's youngest daughter woke him with the news. Tanya rushed into the bedroom of their dacha at Arkhangelskoye shouting "Papa, get up! There's a coup!"

"That's illegal!" Boris said, still groggy with sleep. Tanya told him all the details she knew of the Emergency Committee's strange announcements, and of the men behind the plot. Yeltsin could not believe his ears.

"Are you kidding?" he said as he got up, still trying to make sense of the overnight government takeover.[2] But he knew, of course, that she was not joking. No daughter of Boris Yeltsin's would joke about a mortal threat to the Soviet

Union, and perhaps their family's lives as well.

Boris knew he must get to Moscow. But first, he had to make certain he would not be arrested, or shot, before he could act. He called the commander of the Soviet paratroop forces. General Pavel Grachev reported that a member of the Emergency Committee had ordered his division into Moscow. Grachev made it clear to Yeltsin—and later to the Emergency Committee—that his loyalty was with Gorbachev. "Don't worry," Grachev said. "I will provide you with security no matter what."[3]

However, no assurance from a Soviet commander could soothe the fears of Boris's wife and family. When they saw him donning a bullet proof vest over his brown suit, Naya and Tanya tried to talk him out of going to Moscow.

"What are you trying to protect with that bullet-proof vest?" Naya asked. "Your head is still unprotected. And your head is the main thing."[4]

Tanya could not repress an awful premonition. "I had the horrible, impossible thought that perhaps I was seeing Papa for the last time."[5] Still, family members could rarely talk Boris out of anything. And they knew they could be in danger, too, if they stayed at the dacha. After Boris left, the women, grandchildren and Tanya's husband Lyosha, along with a group of bodyguards, made their own escape.

Boris sped to the White House, even as columns of armored personnel carriers bore down on Moscow. Over the next several hours, he and his staff pieced together the hidden story behind the attempted coup.

The Emergency Committee members had ambushed Gorbachev in his lavish vacation mansion on the Crimea late in the afternoon of the previous day, August 18, 1991. A motorcade of limousines and black Volga escort cars had passed through the main gate of the palace-like main house. Gorbachev had picked up one of his many phones. The line was dead. He had picked up another receiver. Silence. Someone had cut the lines. Gorbachev knew the danger might be urgent or even fatal.

But the group of Emergency Committee members he found sitting in his office did not want Gorbachev's life. They wanted his power—and his cooperation.

One of Gorbachev's top assistants headed up the Emergency Committee. A neat, bespectacled aide, Chief of Staff Valery Boldin, had served as Gorbachev's right hand man. Boldin, who owed his career to Gorbachev now spoke for the coup plotters in demanding his boss' resignation.

Gorbachev tried to persuade the conspirators that they faced defeat if they attempted a return to hard-line Communist rule. But they refused to accept his advice.

"Go to hell!" Gorbachev shouted finally.

Committee members then called in a contingent of guards, who soon took positions along with KGB agents at the chain link fence encircling the compound. While guards carrying Kalashnikov automatic rifles sealed off the perimeter of the president's summer home, the Emergency Committee prepared their next step. Phones rang in the homes of Soviet media chiefs in the middle of the night, and they were summoned to their newspaper, television or radio posts. They soon found instructions for the first of a series of bewildering announcements on their desks.

Gorbachev had been under house arrest for more than twelve hours when Boris' staff gathered at 8:15 Monday morning to draft an official statement of resistance against the coup. While leaders throughout the republic wondered what to do, Yeltsin's group took a forceful stand against the Emergency Committee in the first, critical hours.

Yeltsin, along with Alexander Rutskoi, and Supreme Soviet Speaker Ruslan Khasbulatov, signed a handwritten statement calling for an immediate general strike by the nation's workers. The group then gathered in the White House to further clarify their stand. They wrote out ten demands, which included Gorbachev's immediate release, a medical checkup for Gorbachev, and for restored freedom of the press. In addition, they rejected all orders issued by the Emergency Committee.

Boris reads a statement of defiance from the top of an armed personnel carrier during the failed coup on August 19, 1991. (AP/Wide World)

Yeltsin called a press conference inside the White House to condemn the coup; he was the first leader in the USSR to do so. Then he marched out to meet the mob gathered in the street.

Some later said that Yeltsin looked nervous as he marched down the White House steps. But if he was, he soon recovered his nerve, as he climbed onto the top of a tank to deliver a speech. Now it was his bodyguards' turn to worry, as they surveyed the armored might of the conspirators who had ordered up thousands of troops. A forest of tank barrels were aimed at the White House.

"Citizens of Russia . . . Yeltsin said. "We are dealing with a rightist, reactionary, anti-constitutional coup. Accordingly, we proclaim all decisions and instructions of this committee to be unlawful. We appeal to citizens of Russia to give fitting rebuff to the putchists and demand a return of the country to normal, constitutional development.[6]

"Soldiers, officers and generals, the clouds of terror and dictatorship are gathering over the whole country," he shouted. "They must not be allowed to bring eternal night."[7]

To some, Yeltsin looked like a desperate man as he stood atop the tank. Some thought his words to be the last gasp of democracy, and waited for the tanks to crush *glasnost* and *perestroika*. Yet the speech from the tank proved to be Yeltsin's finest hour.

Boris, characteristically, seized the moment, while other Soviet leaders cowered or rode the fence. His critics had often scoffed at Yeltsin's claims to stand on principle, his blustering style, and his self-promoted image as a warrior. But even they could not easily dismiss the courage of a Russian leader who denounced the plotters while looking down the Emergency Committee's gun barrels. News cameras caught the image of Yeltsin's speech and flashed it around the nation and the world. He became a symbol of the popular rebellion which soon rose up against the coup, as Soviet citizens fought back against dictatorship for the first time in the history of the republic.

For once, word of mouth outraced the electronic media. A KGB agent told General Oleg Kalugin, who had spoken to the crowd after Yeltsin, that a horde of demonstrators was headed toward the street where Kalugin had parked his car. Hoping to get his vehicle out of their way, Kalugin instead ran almost headlong into the protesters. He was lucky, though. Many had heard the speech he had made that promised, "We are not going to shoot the president of Russia," and knew he was on their side.[8] They asked him to lead them back to the White House. To his astonishment, this career army officer found himself leading a crowd of more than a thousand anti-government protesters chanting through the streets.

In a matter of minutes, the mood in Moscow had changed from resigned defeatism to determined defiance. Emboldened by the scene in front of the White House, masses of people surged into the streets throughout the day. They, too, found the courage to defy the tanks. Columns of armor poured into the capital at 1 p.m. to support the coup plotters, but they could not keep the crowd from growing. By 3 p.m., most city intersections were jammed with people, tanks, soldiers and cars. By dusk, several thousand stood in front of the White House, defying military orders to disperse. Other crowds scattered throughout the city numbering in the tens of thousands.

More amazing than the spontaneous crowds were the mutinies which flared up within the ranks of the Army, Navy and Air Force. Boris had wisely made friends with high ranking military officials, and now they came to his aid. In addition to Kalugin, several other generals refused to follow the Committee's orders. Ten tanks of the crack Taman Division, for example, defected to Yeltsin, and turned their guns against the troops supporting the Emergency Committee. When the hardliners threatened to send helicopters over the White House, Air Force General Yevgeny Shaposhnihov warned them he would scramble the helicopters with fighter planes. One Russian naval captain defiantly put his vessel out to sea flying the pre-Communist Russian flag, in sympathy with the protesters.

Most ominously for the Emergency Committee, KGB agents ordered to takeover key installations refused to do so. The rebellion of the KGB was a particularly stinging rebuke to KGB chief Vladimir Kryuchkov, who had led the planning for the coup.

Throughout the day, world leaders tried to make sense of the situation in the Soviet Union. They had little success the first day. The Emergency Committee had stopped all communication to Gorbachev. Instead, they offered to talk to foreign leaders themselves. However, their offer was not accepted.

The Emergency Committee showed itself to the nation, and the world, for the first time at 6 PM on August 19, 1991. Vice-President Yanayev took the podium at the Foreign Ministry Press Center. The assembled camera crews and reporters immediately noticed something very strange about this puffy-faced man who supposedly had taken control of one of the world's superpowers.

Yanayev twitched nervously, and his hands shook as he read a prepared statement. He told the press corp the committee had seized power to prevent the breakup of the USSR, and promised to quickly restore order, stop the violence, and stamp out the criminal underworld. But his words sounded more like outdated Communist propaganda slogans.

Clearly not prepared for the trap he was stepping into, Yanayev opened the floor for questions. The angry foreign press was aggressive and urgent with its questions.

"Where is Mikhail Sergevich Gorbachev?" asked Carroll Bogert, a foreign correspondent for *Newsweek* magazine. "What is he sick with? Specifically, concretely, what disease does he have?"[9] Yanayev explained Gorbachev was still on vacation, and undergoing treatment for "an illness." Reporters sensed a timid note in Yanayev's reply.

The reporters continued to fire indignant questions. Did the plotters realize they pulled off a military coup? Did they plan to go ahead with full-scale censorship? The media response frightened the men of the Emergency Committee, and further weakened their will. These were Party members who had cut their political teeth during the Brezhnev era, when such disrespect could have been silenced with imprisonment. Now, confronted with the task of meeting reasonable questions with reasonable answers, the Committee's answers were unconvincing.

News of the Committee's weak performance flashed throughout the world, along with rumors, that later turned out to be true, that Yanayev had taken refuge in his office, where he steadily consumed bottle after bottle of vodka, soon ended any chance the conspirators may have had of gaining international legitimacy. Western leaders issued separate statements on the coup, but their condemnation of the Emergency Committee was unanimous.

The storm of rebellion soon swept through the other republics of the USSR. Siberian coal miners threw down their picks and shovels in a show of support for the coup resisters. In other parts of the Soviet Union, 200,000 people marched to the Winter Palace in Leningrad, where a similar revolt in 1917 had lain the foundations of Soviet Communism.[10]

Yeltsin, and other speakers electrified a crowd of about 200,000 on Tuesday, August 20. He spoke from the second floor balcony of the White House. The crowds, filled with teenagers and adults too young to remember the horrors of Stalin's time, thrilled at the sight of the nation's leaders joining them in an act of valiant defiance. Yeltsin told them not to back down from the "junta," his derogatory name for the coup conspirators. "We will hold out as long as we must, to remove this junta from power," Yeltsin shouted.

"We will win!" the crowd chanted in agreement.[11]

The anti-coup rebellion spread with every hour. Television news directors stepped up coverage of the public resistance, despite the Emergency Committee directive to block it out. One KGB officer at a station lifted a vodka toast with the head of the television division to signal his willingness to allow the truth to be broadcast. The Committee intensified its intimidation campaign, sending trucks with loudspeakers to warn the crowd at the White House of an impending military assault. The protesters responded by tearing up cobblestones, gathering bricks and planks to build barricades, while others blocked the streets with buses.

After nightfall, the tension reached a near-breaking point. Ninety men formed three rows of a human chain across the White House steps. A Russian Orthodox priest read the Lord's prayer in blessing. Ten women lined up in the rain across the eight traffic lanes of Kutovsky Prospect with a sign reading "Soldiers, don't shoot your mothers!"[12]

The first violence erupted shortly before midnight, when shots rang out from Garden Ring Road near the American Embassy. One of the soldiers had broken under the stress and began firing into the demonstrators. Three people were killed and the crowd went crazy, shouting "Fascists! Shame! Shame!"[13]

The personnel carriers tried to retreat, but civilians blocked their line of escape by driving water trucks across their path. Some Russian legislators worked to keep the violence from escalating, pleading with the crowd and riding the tops of tanks filled with frightened young soldiers.

Meanwhile, Yeltsin's advisor Ruslan Khasbulatov demanded answers from the plotters over the telephone. Did they plan to storm the White House or not? Defense Minister Dmitry Yazov refused to give a straight answer.

KGB strongman Vladimir Kryuchkov, one of the masterminds of the plot, finally gave his assurances that there would not be an attack that night. "You can sleep soundly," Kryuchkov told the men in the White House.[14] The Committee's guns remained silent.

The next morning, the Emergency Committee was faced with a simple, but terrifying, dilemma. The only way for the coup to succeed would be through violence. The White House would have to be attacked, the leaders of the resistance shot or jailed. Even more troubling to the increasingly timid men gathered in the Kremlin was the possibility of different factions within the armed forces fighting each other. They had started the coup expecting the people, and the opposition's leaders, to quietly give up. That was what had happened before, when Khrushchev was toppled in 1964; when the reform communists in Czechoslovakia were driven out of office by Soviet tanks in 1968; and when martial law had been declared in Poland in 1981. Then, the hardliners had simply announced a coup had taken place, and that was that.

But this time it was different. They had not counted on the courage and sheer bravado of Boris Yeltsin. With a single speech, Yeltsin had undermined the hardliner's neat scenario. Now they were faced with a decision: either open fire and turn the streets of Moscow into a battlefield, or give up.

The Emergency Committee signaled its answer just after one o'clock on Wednesday afternoon, August 21, 1991. The Defense Ministry ordered all troops to leave Moscow. The coup had failed.

The soldiers, and their commanders, most of whom had been reluctant warriors, happily obeyed. Joyous crowds cheered as the armored vehicles rumbled back to their bases; many soldiers cheered back.

At 2:15 p.m., Yeltsin told the Russian parliament that the plotters were en route to Vnukovo Airport in an escape attempt. Vice-President Alexander Rutskoi gave chase. Rutskoi also led an expedition to Gorbachev's Crimean vacation home to rescue the Soviet President. Several of the plotters arrived at Gorbachev's Foros dacha, wanting to explain their actions, and perhaps receive an official reprieve. Gorbachev refused to see them. Instead, he had them arrested by his guard, now confident that they held the upper hand against the Committee's agents.

Back in Moscow but exhausted from the ordeal, Gorbachev did not meet with the demonstrators, but went straight home. He did not realize he was making the first of several political mistakes that would lead to his downfall.

Over the next several days, police arrested the plotters. One of them, Soviet Interior Minister Boris Pugo, committed suicide.

Ironically, Gorbachev soon found himself among the political casualties. He might have expected to return as a conquering hero. Boris Yeltsin knew better, and quickly erased the notion from Gorbachev's mind. For years, Yeltsin had thought Gorbachev's judgement was slipping. Yeltsin could not understand why Gorbachev turned against his natural allies, the reformers, and sought support in the old-style hardline Communists who had eventually turned against him. The failed coup had vindicated Yeltsin's doubts about Gorbachev, and had given him the long-awaited chance to topple Gorbachev from power.

It took some time before Gorbachev realized everything had changed. In a press conference on August 22, the day after the coup collapsed, he defended the Communist Party. The reality of the new political dynamic that existed in his country only became clear to him when he entered the halls of the Russian White House to thank his rescuers. Gorbachev even seemed to think it was his moment of supreme triumph. But he received a rude surprise.

When Gorbachev began speaking from a prepared text delegates interrupted the nationally-televised speech by shouting their objections to Communism.

Yeltsin then accused Gorbachev of having surrounded himself with his worst enemies and revealing a dangerous blindness of political judgment. Yeltsin then produced a document which Gorbachev had not seen. It was the record of a Monday meeting of Gorbachev's handpicked cabinet. The meeting had been called by the leaders of the coup, and they had demanded to know from each minister if they supported the Emergency Committee. All but two of Gorbachev's own ministers had supported the plotters.[15]

Yeltsin was far from finished with his humiliation of Gorbachev, and his attack on the Soviet Union as it then existed. At this dramatic moment, Yeltsin made it clear for the entire world to see that he now considered himself a citizen of Russia, and not a comrade of the Soviet Union.

With a tight little smile, he flashed another document. "On a lighter note," he said, "shall we now sign a decree suspending the activities of the Russian Communist Party?"[16] The room broke into applause. Gorbachev's bewildered and muttered objections were ignored.

Gorbachev finally realized he was beaten, as was the Communist Party. On Saturday, Gorbachev destroyed the last vestiges of the party's power before resigning himself. He handed the Party's property over to the government, and banned Party involvement in any government agency or branch of the armed services. These measures demolished the Party's entire network of control.

Over the next weeks, the country went into a frenzy of toppling the public relics of Communism. In cities throughout Russia, statues of Lenin and Stalin were toppled. People had their pictures taken sitting on the broken stone heads of these former heroes of the USSR.

Yeltsin rushed the Soviet Union to a quick death by sending a delegation to the Ukraine to sign a document that sealed them in an alliance that existed outside the Soviet system. This new partnership included two-thirds of the population in what had formerly been the Soviet Union. Moreover, they extended an invitation to other former Soviet Republics to join them. This was the beginning of the creation of the new, looser alliance that came to be called the Commonwealth of Independent States.

The number of republics declaring independence quickly swelled to fifteen. On September 2, 1991, the Congress of People's Deputies voted to dissolve the Soviet Union.

For a while, Gorbachev hung on in a sort of twilight zone. After failing to salvage some kind of remnant of the old Soviet Union, he realized all his efforts were futile. His final surrender came on Christmas Day. In a speech tinged with bitterness, he announced his resignation, and formally declared an end to the Union of Soviet Socialist Republics. All power was given to the new Commonwealth of Independent States. He did not try to cover up his resentment at being forced out of office, but acknowledged that history had indeed left the Soviet Union behind. "We're now living in a new world," Gorbachev said.[17]

With that, the architect of *perestroika* and *glasnost* went into retirement. He would later emerge as Yeltsin's critic, bringing the wheel full circle. Western leaders and media lauded the last leader of the USSR as he stepped down, recalling how much he had done to bring his country out of the darkness of tyranny. In his own nation, where his popularity ratings had fallen to abysmal lows, it would take Russians a little longer to give him his due.

The country was still infatuated with its new leader, the hero of the coup resistance. Yeltsin's star shone brightly for a few months. But the grace period quickly ended, as Yeltsin grappled with the new government's staggering problems. Now the yoke of responsibility lay firmly on the Russian

President's shoulders. The road to democracy would not be easy. Boris Yeltsin had not seen the last of controversy, nor had the streets of Moscow seen the last of soldiers, tanks and blood.

ELEVEN

THE SEIGE
OF PARLIAMENT

Euphoria had gripped the Russian people during the days of the coup, as they realized ordinary citizens could now change the government. Even as the plotters went to their jail cells and the tanks rolled back to their bases, some protesters continued their public demonstration by spray painting anti-KGB slogans on the walls of the once-dreaded police agency. The city declared August 30 as Moscow Day. Fireworks exploded over the capital and musicians staged the first-ever rock concert in the shadow of the Kremlin Wall.

For the moment, Boris Yeltsin was more popular than any rock star. He had shown his toughness and courage at the right time, stamping his image on the rebellion with a defiant fist. But he soon discovered the fleeting nature of such fame.

When the music, cheers and fireworks subsided, an unsettling realization settled on the Russian people. They had watched, both on television and first hand, as the Soviet empire crashed. It had taken only weeks before Gorbachev signed its official death certificate.

Earlier empires had taken decades, even centuries, to fall. The Soviet Union disappeared in weeks. The realization left even ardent anti-communist reformers a bit shell-shocked.

For communists and others with strong nationalist feelings, a sense of humiliation smoldered in the ruins of the Soviet Union. It was no longer an established power slowly making its way down the road of reform, as in Gorbachev's reign, but a new nation making up its rules as it went along. Everything had changed. Nothing could be taken for granted. This was the world President Yeltsin inherited.

Boris even had to discover that in this new world even old allies could become enemies. Vice-President Alexander Rutskoi and Parliament Speaker Ruslan Khasbulatov had stood solidly with Yeltsin throughout the failed coup. But, in a matter of months, they would turn on the President and become his bitterest enemies as Yeltsin attempted to introduce radical reforms into the Russian economy and political structure.

In 1991, Russia had a form of government structured similarly to the government in France. The office of president was the top executive office, and was voted on by the entire Russian people. It was the most powerful position in the government.

There was also a vice-president, whose role was ill-defined. During the 1991 election, Yeltsin had chosen Alexander Rutskoi to be his running mate. He would soon become his most bitter opponent.

In addition to president vice-president was the position of Premier. In the Russian system, the Premier was responsible for day-to-day operations of the government, which included working closely with the Congress. Because of his close relationship with the deputies, the body was given the right to vote their approval, or disapproval, of whomever the president selected to be Premier. It was a procedure similar to the way Justices to the Supreme Court are appointed and approved in the United States.

The last election for the Congress of People's Deputies had been held in 1989, before the failed coup and the dissolution of the Soviet Union. The Communist Party had controlled the election apparatus in 1989, so the results did not reflect the true wishes of the Russian people. Many of these deputies, perhaps as many as 80%, were members of the Communist Party.[1] While most in the Congress had not supported the coup plotters, they, in turn, were not ready to overthrow the entire communist system. Many were reform communists, similar to Gorbachev. These deputies looked on in dismay as Yeltsin made it clear he intended to convert the economy to a western-style, market-driven system. They eagerly searched for leaders to help them stop Yeltsin's reforms.

In short, the period after the fall of the Soviet Union was politically chaotic. Representative government was a new idea in Russia. The citizenry were being asked to participate in a procedure with which they had little experience. In addition, after the coup many political leaders, especially Rutskoi and Khasbulatov, thought it was the ideal time for them to gain power at Yeltsin's expense. Rutskoi and Khasbulatov were Russian nationalists, who still held deep antagonisms for the old enemies of the cold war years, such as the United States, and were quick to find fault with the former Soviet republics that made up the Commonwealth of Independent States. They also saw themselves as defenders of the Russians in the former republics who had previously held elite positions but felt like foreigners. The Congress rang with speeches demanding Yeltsin to invade this republic or that republic in retaliation for some slight against Russia.

Yeltsin admitted later he made a mistake in not restructuring the political system before beginning economic reforms.[2] But he was in a great hurry to reform the economy. He wanted to give Russians something as potent as national pride: spending power and a higher standard of living. He wanted an American-style free market economy. Boris had had enough of the old system, which had controlled most of the property in the country and tried to manage the entire economy from offices in the Kremlin. He had seen the prosperity in America, the result of a free market economy in which companies could produce whatever customers wanted, and people could buy whatever they could afford. He wanted to bring the lessons of the U.S., a land he considered an economic paradise compared to his own country.

But, in order to accomplish this goal, Boris needed to keep tight control of an increasingly divided government. And he failed in this task. He failed by relying too much on his popularity, and by not building a solid political base, before beginning the economic changes. At the same time he was attempting to overthrow 70 years of economic stagnation, his foes in parliament were able to make simple appeals to bruised Russian pride, and to attack the upheaval caused by economic reform.

The economic reform that Yeltsin attempted has come to becalled "shock therapy." This simply means change the system as quickly as possible, and to avoid any of the partial steps that Gorbachev had favored. Auction off the communal farms to the people. Force state-run businesses to sell stock on the open market, and to make a profit or go bankrupt. End government subsidies to the thousands of unproductive parts of the economy. The theory was that changing the system quickly would, in the long run, result in less suffering for the citizens. However, in the short run shock therapy created great economic chaos.

Within weeks, millions of Russians were unemployed. These unemployed workers had no money to purchase the property, especially the land, that the government was selling. Therefore, those with money, who were for the most part former Communist Party officials, were able to grab up vast amounts of wealth for a fraction of its value.

Shock therapy also set off inflation. Every day the ruble bought less than it did before. When Boris tried to slow inflation by devaluing the ruble, many Russians discovered that their paper money, as well as any pensions they might have, were worthless. Goods began disappearing off the shelves of state-owned stores because the new wealthy could afford to pay higher prices in private boutiques. In the old days people had stood in line to buy bread. Now, they stood in line, only to discover that there was no bread on the shelves.

And, perhaps most galling, some people did get rich. But the people who got rich were, for the most part, those who were better off financially to begin with. It was a classic case of the rich getting richer, and the poor getting poorer. Yeltsin's popularity began slipping, and his enemies in the Congress seized on every opportunity to blame him for all the problems.

Ironically, there were political reasons why shock therapy was attractive to Yeltsin. He knew he might have only a short time to alter Russia. There was certain to be a reaction, a period when people would look back fondly on the days of guaranteed jobs and housing, and would forget all the bad things about the old system. He wanted to change quickly so that he could change more deeply. And finally, Yeltsin was simply not temperamentally suited for a 'go slow' approach.

Adding to his problems was that, for the first time, Yeltsin was no longer the outsider. No one viewed him as an underdog. Yet, in actuality, he held far less power than had Gorbachev, and his opponents in Congress tried constantly to strip him of the power he did wield. Khasbulatov, for example, talked continually of impeachment. Yeltsin survived one attempt to impeach him by only 72 votes.

Seeking a way to release some of the political tension, Yeltsin proposed early elections. His hope was that the elections might unseat many of his critics in the parliament.

Yeltsin supporters claimed that his election plan struck fear in the hearts of Rutskoi, Khasbulatov and their allies. If they lost they would have had to give up their chauffeur-driven Mercedes and their *dachas*. Both men were often accused of standing for nothing but opposition to Yeltsin. But in reality, Khasbulatov and Rutskoi disagreed with Yeltsin's desire for a quick dash to a free market. They argued such a quick transition would only worsen economic woes for the average Russian.

At times during the year after the coup, Yeltsin appeared drained of his old strength. He promised a head-on assault against those who stood in his way when the Russian Congress opened on December 1, 1992. But his keynote address was far from vintage Yeltsin. He wavered between aggressive attacks and offers of reconciliation with his enemies. His speech drew snickers, while Khasbulatov's supporters greeted his speech with resounding applause.

By appearing weak and uncertain, Yeltsin played into enemy hands. They made use of the opportunity by rejecting Yeltsin's nominee to be Premier, Yegor T. Gaidar.

Gaidar was one of the chief architects of shock therapy,

and had been serving as Acting Premier since June. When, on December 9, 1992, Congress rejected Gaidor's confirmation to the post, it was a humiliating set-back for Yeltsin. He further stunned observers by not reacting to the defeat in the old, fiery Yeltsin manner. He simply accepted it, and began looking for someone else to appoint as Premier. Both the defeat in the Congress, and Yeltsin's weak reaction, tarnished his reputation as a political strongman. Perhaps, the years of struggle had temporarily sapped his energy. But his supporters were dismayed. A writer for a pro-reform newspaper wrote that the *glasnost*-era warrior had disappeared, to be replaced by "a person docilely and languidly awaiting the outcome of his fate."[3]

Boris knew he had to find some method to regain public support. Because he had failed to build a political structure, such as a solid party apparatus, only one thing could save his presidency, and the reforms he was convinced Russia desperately needed—his personal popularity. He therefore challenged Congress to hold a public referendum in April of 1993. The referendum would ask the people who they trusted to carry out economic reforms, the Congress or the President.

The Congress could not ignore Yeltsin's challenge. It reluctantly agreed to the referendum.

The public vote offered Boris the opportunity to regain

the political momentum. As he had done so many times before, Yeltsin took his campaign to the streets. He called on average people and laborers to support him. He shook hands with workers in a Moscow auto factory. But no longer did the mere sight of Yeltsin spark manic enthusiasm, as it had in the days when the public saw him as a rebel. A woman in the factory said she definitely planned to support Yeltsin—because he was "the lesser of two evils."[4] This was a common sentiment.

The public was divided on the subject of Yeltsin. In one demonstration, one group carried signs reading WE'RE WITH YOU, BORIS! While on the other side of the street posters proclaimed YELTSIN AND COMPANY ARE ROBBING US! A corps of police officers nervously kept the peace. Confrontations like this occurred frequently as the country prepared to cast its ballots.[5] An anti-Yeltsin rally in February drew a crowd of 20,000 people.

The battle on the floor of Congress raged throughout the referendum campaign. Time and again, Yeltsin watched as the electronic screen in the Kremlin hall flashed *ne prinyato (not approved)* in response to his proposals.

In midst of this intense political struggle Boris suffered a personal tragedy. His beloved mother Klavdia died on March 21, 1993. He was filled with grief; photos showed a weeping President Yeltsin attending the funeral. But the all-important referendum was only a month away, and he had little time for personal suffering.

During the referendum campaign, Yeltsin began to regain the momentum, despite enormous opposition. The public continued to support him over his enemies. A rally on March 28 at St. Basil's Cathedral revived the memory of Yeltsin's charisma. "The time is up for compromise!" Yeltsin roared, and the crowd of 60,000 roared back its approval.[6] On the other side of St. Basil's, a rival group of fascists and communists drew a crowd of less than a quarter of the size of the pro-Yeltsin crowd.

The referendum was held on April 25, 1993, and the voters handed Yeltsin a solid victory: 65% of the voters turned out; 58% expressed confidence in the President; 53% said they supported his economic policies, a stinging rebuke to his critics; 64% said they wanted to see a new election for Congress, compared with 33% who said they wanted an early presidential election.

Parliament Speaker Khasbulatov and Vice-President Rutskoi refused to accept defeat. They defiantly called the entire voting process a "fraud," and dismissed the vote as a public opinion poll.

But on the heels of such a victory, the President was not to be so easily dismissed. He quickly declared an end to

Boris with his wife Naya at his mother's funeral, March 23, 1993. (AP/Wide World)

Vice-President Rutskoi's authority to hold inquiries into the activities of government officials. He then fired two officials who had opposed reforms, including his handpicked head of the state security council, Yuri Skokov. Yeltsin wanted to send a message with the firings: when he said he would sack officials who fought reform, he meant it.

Yeltsin pushed his hand further, demanding a June convention to write a new constitution. Within its opening minutes, the constitutional convention disintegrated into a fiasco. When he failed to get the attention of the delegates for his speech, Speaker Khasbulatov stormed out of the opening session. He gave a news conference in which he called Yeltsin's ideas for a new constitution a "total assault on democracy."

Yeltsin's written draft of the constitution was indeed controversial; it not only called for new Congressional elections in October, but abolished Rutskoi's office of vice-president entirely. One Communist delegate became so incensed he charged the podium, shrieking insults at Yeltsin. He kicked and struggled as security guards carried him from the hall.

By this time, Yeltsin realized he had squandered too many opportunities. It was time to make drastic political changes. As the Congress continued to defy him, he promised a "hot month" in September. After two years of threats and counter-threats, most Russians had no idea how accurate Yeltsin's prophecy would prove.

The Congress played into Yeltsin's hands when they announced their plan to pass a budget on September 22, 1993. The budget was very similar to one which Yeltsin had twice vetoed because it would have triggered rampant inflation. In the same session, anti-reform forces in the Congress decided to approve a slate of bills from the Committee for Constitutional Legislation, a panel chaired by a leader of the neo-fascist National Salvation Front. The proposals would have stripped the president of the right to veto legislation, and would have treated any presidential violation of Congressional decisions as a criminal act. The bills flew directly in the face of the results of the April referendum.In short, the Congress was still determined to strip Yeltsin of all his powers.

Yeltsin knew it was time for decisive action. On the evening of September 21, he announced on television and radio that he was dissolving the Congress. "It is my duty as president to acknowledge that the present legislature has forfeited the right to be at the major levers of power," he said.[7] He called for new Congressional elections to be held on December 11th and 12th, 1993.

The speech caught everyone by surprise, especially Khasbulatov and Rutskoi. They convened members of

On September 21, 1993, Boris announces to the nation that elections
for a new parliament will be held on December 11 and 12, 1993.
(AP/Wide World)

Congress in a "rump session"—a parliamentary meeting
made up of expelled delegates, and passed laws to strip
Yeltsin of his power. Then they swore in Rutskoi as President
of Russia. The group decided to remain in the White House,
as their allies circled the building to provide protection for
the deputies inside.

Superficially, the Congress' actions resembled the events
of August, 1991. But inside the White House, many of the
speeches given by the deputies were the sinister opposite

of the appeals for democracy in 1991. Speakers denounced Yeltsin for, among other alleged sins, taking bribes from Jews, and for selling out Russia to the U.S.-Zionist conspiracy to control the world.

The standoff between Yeltsin and the deputies stretched for thirteen days. Yeltsin, at first attempted peaceful, but tough, measures to deal with the entrenched rebels. He cut off the electricity and the water to the White House. Cordons of armed, helmeted riot police surrounded the building and issued ultimatums for the deputies to leave. But the deadlines passed without results. Next, Yeltsin's forces borrowed a page from American siege tactics and blasted the White House with high decibel rock and rap music. While the renegade lawmakers passed meaningless decrees and called for popular support, the lyrics of the rock band Dire Straits echoed off the white walls.

But the relationship between Yeltsin and the rebels had deteriorated too far for violence to be stemmed. On the afternoon of October 1, hundreds of stone-throwing rebel supporters fought police in central Moscow. A dozen officers fell injured in the battle. Khasbulatov condemned the police from inside the White House, and called for further resistance.

The next day, several dozen hardliners attempted to rebuild the barricades that had been destroyed by the police.

But they were forced to flee. The greatest show of support for the anti-Yeltsin deputies came on October 3, when 10,000 demonstrators gathered under a statue of Soviet founder Vladimir Lenin. Riot police tried to stop the demonstration, only to be overwhelmed by the crowd.

Thirty minutes later, the demonstrators marched to the White House. They crashed the police lines with clubs, pipes and boards, and threw rocks and bottles at the officers. Dozens more policemen were injured. When the demonstrators reached the White House, volleys of gunfire rang out. Volunteer guards commandeered army trucks and stormed a nearby government building.

Despite the violence, Yeltsin expressed confidence in his attempt to break the will of the rebel deputies without bloodshed. "Common sense will prevail," he said.[8]

But common sense failed when Vice-President Rutskoi, speaking from the balcony of the White House on October 3, 1993, he called on his supporters to storm the city's main television complex. The crowds followed his orders; thousands attacked the building. Elite guards, loyal to Yeltsin, held off the attackers. At 6:30 p.m., Yeltsin declared a state of emergency. Three television stations went off the air after demonstrators fired rocket-propelled grenades at the television center. Soon, a fierce gun battle erupted. Dozens of protesters broke into the building, only to be forced out again by the troops inside. Twelve personnel carriers carrying police reinforcements raced to the scene.

All chances for a peaceful resolution had ended. Yeltsin had no choice but to meet violence with violence. The assault on the White House began in earnest the next morning at Moscow's rush hour. Tanks opened fire at seven a.m.

Yeltsin called a cease fire at noon to allow the hardliners inside the burning building a chance to surrender. Seventy-two people, mostly women, filed out with their hands up. Another barrage of gunfire followed the cease fire. Commandoes stormed the building. Soldiers began staking bodies in the street.

Finally, in the late afternoon of October 4, 1993, the last of the weary hardliners surrendered.

"I never thought he would do this," a stunned Khasbulatov told a reporter. "Why isn't anyone coming to help us?"[9] Apparently, the lesson of the April referendum had receded from his memory. Overwhelmingly, most Russians supported Yeltsin.

Yeltsin had regained his image as a strong man by breaking the backs of his most bitter enemies. But criticism of his actions soon followed. Perhaps he was too tough, some Western leaders and journalists speculated. Yeltsin had looked like a hero when he stood up to the Emergency

Committee, and Western leaders sang his praises. But could they continue to embrace a leader who dissolved an elected Congress and assaulted it with tanks? The entire scene was faintly, horribly, reminiscent of the old Soviet Union.

Nonetheless, most Russia watchers, and, most importantly, Russian citizens, sided with Yeltsin. The strange assortment of characters who emerged from the besieged White House—including politicians of the center Communists, extreme nationalists and anti-Jewish race baiters—seemed to justify Yeltsin's harsh methods.

Now, Yeltsin announced, as the flames were being extinguished in the White House, that democracy could move forward to the next stage—the first totally free elections in Russian history. But, in the political campaign to come, Yeltsin would not only feel his extremist enemies breathing behind him. He would see their faces, as they filed for office.

TWELVE

A NEW WORLD

The December election campaign seemed, at times, like a circus with a cast of thousands. Grandmothers, athletes, and pop stars joined conventional politicians on the ballot. On the surface, at least, the rowdy and colorful campaigns appeared to be a much-needed antidote to the political bloodshed of recent months.

President Boris Yeltsin, however, did not participate in the campaign. He asked only for support for the new constitution, also on the ballot, and a measure which would give the president broad powers. Otherwise, he remained unusually silent as everyone from career politicians to dangerous demagogues attacked the status quo.

Those politicians who clearly broadcast their message earned the most success. The largest of the pro-Yeltsin parties was called Russia's Choice, and was led by former Premier Yegor Gaidor. The "Yabloko" Bloc, which wanted to curb inflation and crime, also supported Yeltsin, as did a few smaller, liberal groups. In the political middle were groups which did not promise to support everything Yeltsin requested, but did favor many of his reforms. The Democratic Party of Russia took this middle-of-the-road position, as did the nation's first women's party, Women of Russia.

The most potent threat to Yeltsin and his reforms came from the Communists, most of whom wanted a return to the old order, and the Liberal Democrats, who campaigned openly to eradicate democracy and impose a military dictatorship. The Liberal Democrats were led by Vladimir Zhirinovsky, the 47-year-old lawyer who had run third in the 1991 Russian presidential race. Zhirinovsky promised to rebuild the Russian empire. He also made verbal attacks against Jews and other minorities, and threatened to launch nuclear missiles at any Western country which defied him.

Zhirinovsky quickly earned the title of "the new Hitler" for his racism and his easily tossed-off threats to use nuclear weapons to get what he wanted from the West. Zhirinovsky had written an autobiography, *The Final March South,* which detailed his plans to build a new Russian empire, with Russian armies reclaiming land and ports from the Mediterranean Sea to the Indian Ocean. He had turned to politics as compensation for a miserable youth, Zhirinovsky wrote in his autobiography, during which he had few friends and almost no success in attracting the opposite sex.

Yet few observers, including those in the media, thought Zhirinovsky posed a serious threat. Western reporters focused on the most colorful characters in the race, of which there was no shortage. Lyudmilla Vartazarova, a 55-year old grandmother of four, led a bizarre coalition of socialists, oil executives and Cossacks who wanted a return to monarchy. She lost her place on the ballot when reformers in her group bolted, and deprived her of the 100,000 signatures she needed to run. Among those who also slipped in the race to get on the ballot were Yuri Vlasov, a weightlifting champion of the 1960 Olympic games, who blamed his downfall on an international Jewish conspiracy. The petition process also eliminated other anti-Yeltsin candidates, such as writer Yuri Bondarev, who once compared Gorbachev's reforms to the Nazi assault on Stalingrad.[1]

Gennady Zyuganov, 49-year-old author of the political book *The Drama of Power*, campaigned as a new style of communist. He promised a communist system which would allow multiple parties, free debate and even some free trade. He excited crowds, appealing to the nostalgia of Russian nationalists and older people whose pensions had been drained by the tremendous inflation. He asked hard-hitting questions of Yeltsin's government. How had a former super-power been reduced to a beggar state in two years? Why was a country which had once ranked as one of the five safest to live now as dangerous as a "rusty atom bomb"? And why were the elderly on fixed incomes being shuffled to the side and forgotten?

"They are talking about democracy," Zyuganov said. "And at the same time, they are destroying everything that was created in the country, not for the last 75 years, but for thousands of years." Zyuganov attacked the proposed constitution as well. "The authority is twice that of the French president, and four times that of the United States president. A man cannot use so much power."[2]

Yeltsin mostly ignored any attacks against him. Instead, he reserved his anger for those who opposed the new constitution. He even threatened to ban candidates from state television if they attacked the constitution, a threat which only seemed to justify those who worried about an excess of presidential power.

The election results on December 12, 1993 were a shock to both Yeltsin and the world. Zhirinovsky, whose speeches had grown increasingly bizarre as the campaign continued, won more than 23% of the vote. The Communists and their allies, the Agrarian Party, won an additional 22%, making a powerful block against any reform efforts. Yeltsin's reformers carried only 35% of the seats. That meant that Zhirinovsky's party and the new communists could stop any reforms advocated by Yeltsin.

Yeltsin's major victory was passage of the constitution, the one thing he had campaigned for. A natural question followed on the heels of the new constitution: If Yeltsin lost the presidency, who then would hold the strong powers Yeltsin had gained?

Yegor Gaidor, who had managed Russia Choice by proxy for the absent Yeltsin, admitted Zhirinovsky and other extremists had caught the party by surprise. "Frankly, the fact that he seemed somewhat comic, a kind of Adolf Hitler parody, confused us," Gaidor said. "We failed to fully realize how serious the threat was."[3]

The response of the electorate bewildered Yeltsin. He emerged from his isolation to say that the people had voted against the bad economic conditions, and not in favor of Zhirinovsky and the other extremists. He retracted a pledge to hold early presidential elections, and then made a shocking statement. He said that after he served out the remainder of his term—due to expire in 1996—he would not run again.

"Everyone knows how many blows have fallen to my lot," Yeltsin said. "For one person, it's too much."[4] He promised, in the meantime, to groom a successor.

The Russian newspaper editors gathered for his statement did not know if they should take it at face value. This certainly did not sound like the old fighting Yeltsin. Still, his strange announcement begged the question: If Yeltsin no longer carried the banner, who would?

Some Russians, and other former Soviet citizens, cared little for December's theater of democracy. When the present became too confusing and ambiguous, they looked inward. Many longed for the past. They wanted meaning and order in their lives, perhaps as much as freedom.

Yeltsin's former home province of Sverdlovsk is now called by its pre-1917 name, Yekaterinburg. Just off a busy street there stands a large white wooden cross. This is where Boris Yeltsin followed the orders of the Politburo to bulldoze the czar's death house in 1976.

Yeltsin's bosses wanted him to erase the historical landmark, so people would stop coming to see an embarrassment in Soviet history. But a strange phenomenon has occurred in recent years. The pilgrims have come back.

They range from newlyweds who want to have their picture taken in front of the cross, to those who want to touch it for its allegedly mystical powers. Some claim it cures their ailments, or gives the lame the power to walk. All day long, people walk up to the cross, press their hands against it, and sometimes leave flowers. Many of those who come say they are driven by a desire to feel more "Russian," a longing to retrieve their past.

These were the feelings that Yeltsin's foes tapped so well in the campaign of 1993. Yet it is easier to identify the vague longings for the past than to identify which era of the past Russians would like to return to. Is it the past of the czars? The Soviet Union's as a superpower? Or are they drawn by a hazy nostalgia for something that never was?

Many Russian politicians have learned the Western art of building careers on the vague yearnings of voters. Gennady Zyuganov, the Communist author so successful in his rallies, has done quite well marketing himself as a "new" Communist who believes in some democracy. Vladimir Zhirinovsky has proven himself a grand master at saying something to please everybody. "I am not a fascist," he declared on the morning of his victory, after a campaign of racist slurs and military threats. He has said many things which must sound soothing to the pilgrims who come to the cross at Yekaterinburg. Zhirinovsky says he would pain-lessly rebuild the Russian empire, restoring the military's might while giving students exemptions from the draft. He would make Russia a great power again, without spilling blood. It is hard for Americans to understand how sweet those words sound to a people who had watched their nation tumble from a superpower to a second-rate country in four months.

"Zhirinovsky was elected because of his promises, not because of his ideology," said one public opinion analyst.[5] And he may have been helped with voters because Yeltsin's "shock treatment," with its too-fast pace toward a free market, shocked poor and average Russians the hardest.

The parliament, now called the *Duma*, dealt Yeltsin a quick slap in the face almost as soon as it convened in 1994. It voted to pardon the 1991 members of the Emergency Committee which kidnapped Mikhail Gorbachev, and the former Congress members who had attempted armed revolt against Yeltsin in 1993. The minute he walked out of jail, former Vice-President Alexander Rutskoi regained his political following. Former Speaker of Parliament Ruslan Khasbulatov sounded a bit more weary of public life, and announced he was getting out of politics.

Boris kept his temper—publicly at least—and did not allow the pardons to become a stumbling block to working with the Duma. In his February 24, 1994 state-of-the-nation address—a first for Russia—Yeltsin sounded a conciliatory note. "The time for infighting in our country has been exhausted," he said. After weeks of speculation about his health, the Russian President looked strong and energetic at the rostrum. And he continued his call for more democracy.

"Yes, there is more freedom in our country," Yeltsin said, "but that is not enough. Our task is to make sure there is more justice, more safety, more confidence in today and tomorrow."[6]

Some in the West will never trust Yeltsin, nor any Russian leader. It is true Yeltsin has not been a perfect president, and certainly not a perfect democrat. He has used both charisma and stern government mandates, depending on which suited him. But he has also shown the strength and toughness necessary to govern a giant nation through one of its greatest historic upheavals.

In *Against the Grain*, written before the fall of the Soviet Union, Yeltsin explained why he had supported Mikhail Gorbachev, a leader he secretly considered inadequate. Gorbachev was the only man who could stop the collapse of the party, Yeltsin wrote. "Our right-wingers, unfortunately, fail to understand this," Yeltsin wrote. "They believe that by the old mechanical method of voting by a show of hands they will succeed in turning back the clock."[7]

Now, in this new era, the ultra-nationalists, the "new" communists, and the fascists are showing the same desire to turn back the clock.

"A man must live like a great bright flame and burn as

brightly as he can," Yeltsin once said. "In the end, he burns out. But this is better than a mean little flame."[8] Yet democracy must outlast the span of a single human life if a country is to prosper under it. Future generations will not determine Boris Yeltsin's place in history by the brightness of his own flame. All that will matter is whether the fire he lit for democracy in Russia will continue to burn.

NOTES

CHAPTER ONE: FARM BOY

[1] Boris Yeltsin. Against the Grain. (New York: Summit Books, 1990), p.22.

[2] Boris Yeltsin. Boris Yeltsin: The Struggle for Russia. (New York: Random House, Inc., 1994) p. 93.

[3] Gwyneth Huges and Simon Welfare. Red Empire: The New Forbidden History of the USSR (New York: St. Martin's Press, 1990), p.94.

[4] Yeltsin, Against the Grain, p.28.

[5] Ibid, p. 27.

[6] David Remnick. Lenin's Tomb: The Last Days of the Soviet Empire. (New York: Random House, Inc., 1993), p. 435.

[7] Yeltsin, Against the Grain, p.28.

[8] Ibid, p. 33.

CHAPTER TWO: FACTORY BOSS

[1] Yeltsin, Against the Grain, p. 95.

[2] Yeltsin, The Struggle for Russia, p. 4.

[3] Yeltsin, Against the Grain, p. 4.

[4] Yale Richmond. From Nyet to Da: Understanding the Russians. (Yarmouth, Maine: Intercultural Press, Inc., 1992), p. 122.

[5] Yeltsin, Against the Grain, p. 50.

[6] William J. Miller, Henry L. Roberrts, Marshall D. Shulman. The Meaning of Communism. (Morristown, N.J.: Silver Burdett Company/Time, Inc., 1963), p. 118.

[7] Yeltsin, Against the Grain, p. 51.

CHAPTER THREE:PROVINCE CHIEF

[1] Yeltsin, Against the Grain, p. 62.

[2] Ibid, p. 63.

[3] Yeltsin, The Struggle for Russia, p. 235.

[4] Yeltsin, Against the Grain, p. 69.

[5] Ibid, pp. 69-70.

[6] Remnick, Lenin's Tomb, p. 153.

CHAPTER FOUR: SOLDIER FOR THE PARTY

[1] Yeltsin, Against the Grain, p. 81.

CHAPTER FIVE: THE CALL TO MOSCOW

[1] Yeltsin, The Struggle for Russia, p. 160.

[2] Yeltsin, Against the Grain, p. 92.

[3] Robert G. Kaiser. Why Gorbachev Happened: His Triumphs and His Failures. (New York: Simon & Schuster, 1991), p. 165.

[4] Yeltsin, Against the Grain, p. 100.

[5] Ibid, p. 129.

CHAPTER SIX: THE PEOPLE'S CHAMPION

[1] John Morrison. Boris Yeltsin: From Bolshevik to Democrat. (New York: Dutton, 1991), p. 43.

[2] Yeltsin, Against the Grain, p. 109.

[3] Ibid, p. 110.

[4] Kaiser, Why Gorbachev Happened, p. 165.

[5] Ibid, p. 167

[6] Yeltsin, Against the Grain, p. 129.

CHAPTER SEVEN: THE "YELTSIN AFFAIR"

[1] Yeltsin, Against the Grain, p. 181.

[2] Ibid, p. 184.

[3] Ibid, p. 191.

[4] Ibid, p. 186.

[5] Morrison, From Bolshevik to Democrat, p. 67.

[6] Ibid, p. 67-68.

[7] Yeltsin, Against the Grain, p. 198.

[8] Ibid, p. 199.

[9] Morrison, From Bolshevik to Democrat, p. 70-71

[10] Ibid, p. 71.

CHAPTER EIGHT: TRIUMPH IN EXILE

[1] Yeltsin, Against the Grain, p. 81.

[2] Morrison, From Bolshevik to Democrat, p. 81.

[3] Yeltsin, The Struggle for Russia, p. 5.

[4] Morrison, From Boshevik to Democrat, p. 81.

[5] Hedrick Smith. The New Russians. (New York: Random House, Inc., 1990), p. 449.

CHAPTER NINE: PRESIDENT YELTSIN

[1] Yeltsin, Against the Grain, p. 244.

[2] Ibid, p. 244.

[3] Ibid, p. 245.

[4] Ibid, p. 246.

[5] Morrison, From Bolshevik to Democrat, p. 98.

[6] Ibid, p. 102.

[7] Ibid, p. 105.

[8] Ibid, 106.

[9] Ibid, p. 104.

[10] Ibid, p. 106.

[11] Gennady Gerasimov (author interview, January 27, 1994).

[12] Yeltsin, Struggle for Russia, p. 31.

[13] Patrick J. Buchanan. "Waiting in the Wings in Moscow." July 30, 1993.

[14] Morrison, From Bolshevik to Democrat, p. 106.

[15] Ibid, p. 269.

[16] Yeltsin, Struggle for Russia, p. 38.

CHAPTER TEN: THE AUGUST COUP

[1] Stuart H. Loory and Ann Imse. Seven Days that Shook the World: The Collapse of Soviet Communism. (Atlanta: Turner Publishing, Inc., 1991) p. 78.

[2] Yelstin, The Strugle for Russia, p. 54.

[3] Loory and Imse, Seven Days, p. 79.

[4] Yeltsin, The Struggle for Russia, p. 42.

[5] Ibid, p. 42.

[6] Loory and Imse, Seven Days, p. 90.

[7] Morrison, From Bolshevik to Democrat, pp.283-284.

[8] Loory and Imse, Seven Days, p. 90.

[9] Ibid, p. 98.

[10] George C. Church. "Anatomy of a Coup. *Time*, Sept. 2, 1991, p. 38.

[11] Loory and Imse, Seven Days, p. 134.

[12] Ibid, p. 135.

[13] Church, Anatomy of a Coup," *Time*, p. 43.

[14] Loory and Imse, Seven Days, p. 158.

[15] Ibid, 159.

[16] Francis X. Clines. "Gorbachev, Last Soviet Leader, Resigns. *The New York Times*, Dec. 26, 1991.

[17] Ibid.

CHAPTER ELEVEN: THE SIEGE OF PARLIAMENT

[1] James Carney. "Yeltsin's Enemies," *Time*, March 9, 1992, p47.

[2] Ibid, p. 49.

[3] Facts on File, Dec. 10, 1992, Vol. 52, p. 915.

[4] Carroll Bogert. "Yeltsin Bets the House," *Newsweek*, Dec. 21, 1992, p. 48.

[5] Ibid, p. 48.

[6] Asking Silly Questions, *The Economist*, April 9, 1993, p. 51.

[7] "Russia Turns Its Back on Parliament," *The Economist*, Sept. 25, 1992, p. 57.

[8] George Rodrigue, *Dallas Morning News*, Oct. 4, 1993.

[9] Howard Witt and James P. Gallagher, *Chicago Tribune*, Oct. 5, 1993.

CHAPTER TWELVE: A NEW WORLD

[1] Keven Fadarko. "A Parliament of Poets, Priests and Rock Stars," *Time*, Nov. 29, 1993, p. 42.

[2] Stephen Seplow. Knight-Ridder Newspapers, Dec. 12, 1993.

[3] George Rodrigue. *Dallas Morning News*, Dec. 12, 1993.

[4] Sergei Shargorsky. *Associated Press,* Oct. 12, 1993.

[5] George Rodrigue. *Dallas Morning News*, Dec. 12, 1993.

[6] Julia Rubin. *Associated Press*, Feb. 25, 1994.

[7] Yeltsin, Against the Grain, p. 262.

[8] Morrison, From Bolshevik to Democrat, p. 292.

CHRONOLOGY

February 1, 1931—Boris Nikoloyevich Yeltsin born in Butko, Sverdlovsk, in the eastern part of the Russian republic, USSR.

1951-55—Studies Civil Engineering at the Urals Polytechnic Intstitute.

1955—Goes to work for the Urals Heavy Pipe Construction Trust.

1956—Marries Naya Girina.

1957—Daughter Lena is born.

1959—Daughter Tanya is born.

1961—Joins the Communist Party USSR.

1976—Receives surprise promotion to Communist Party position of First Secretary of Sverdlovsk Province. This makes Boris the most powerful man in the province.

1981—Elected to the Central Committee of the Soviet Communist Party.

1985—New Soviet leader Mikhail Gorbachev promotes Yeltsin to Central Committee Secretary. Later in the year Boris becomes chairman of the Moscow City Committee.

1986—Elected to the Politburo, the inner circle of power in the Soviet Union.

October 21, 1987—Yeltsin shocks the nation by attacking the Communist Party and its leaders at a meeting of the Central Committee. He offers his resignation. This later became known as the "Yeltsin Affair."

November 11, 1987—Boris is dragged from his hospital bed to be publicly humiliated at a Moscow City Committee meeting, where his resignation is accepted.

March 26, 1989—Yeltsin wins a seat in the new Congress of People's Deputies.

May, 1990-Becomes chairman of the Russian Supreme Soviet.

July, 1990—Yeltsin resigns from the Communist Party.

June 12, 1991—Boris Yeltsin becomes the first democratically elected President of the Russian Republic.

August, 1991—Boris and other democrats successfully resist a coup attempt by Communist hardliners.

December, 1991—The Soviet Union is dissolved and replaced with the new Commonwealth of Independent States.

January, 1992—Yeltsin begins so-called "Shock Therapy," an attempt to rapidly create a market economy in Russia.

March 21, 1993—Yeltsin's mother Klavdia dies.

September 21, 1993—Yeltsin dissolves the Congress of People's Deputies, and calls for elections for a new Congress to be held on December 11 and 12, 1993.

October 3-4, 1993—Yeltsin orders the army to attack the Russian White House, where his political opponents have refused to dissolve the Congress.

December 12, 1993—Elections for a new parliament, the Duma, are held. Yeltsin's political enemies score a sizable victory. The voters also agree to a new constitution giving the President of Russia broader powers.

GLOSSARY

Apparatchiks—Former Communist Party functionaries and bureaucrats.

Communist Party—The party that controlled all aspects of Soviet life from 1917 until 1991.

Duma—The name of the new parliament elected in the December, 1993.

General Secretary—The most powerful position in the Soviet Communist Party. Gorbachev held this position while Yeltsin was President of Russia.

Glasnost—Russian word for "openness." Glasnost was a policy of liberalization on intellectual and personal freedom started by Soviet Leader Mikhail Gorbachev and supported by Yeltsin.

KGB—The Soviet secret police. The KGB was responsible for both foreign and domestic spying.

Perestroika—Russian word for restructuring. A policy of gradual economic reform started by Gorbachev.

Politburo—The inner circle of power in the Soviet Union, composed of a group of approximately 20 of the highest ranking members of the Communist Party of the USSR.

Shock Therapy—The plan to rapidly change the Russian economy from a centrally planned system to an open market system.

SELECTED BIBLIOGRAPHY

Huges, Gwyneth and Simon Welfard, *Red Empire: The New Forbidden History of the USSR* (New York: St. Martin's Press, 1990)

Kaiser, Robert G., *Why Gorbachev Happened: His Triumphs and His Failures* (New York: Simon & Schuster, 1991)

Loory, Stuart H. and Ann Imse, *Seven Days that Shook the World: The Collapse of Soviet Communism* (Atlanta: Turner Publishing, 1991)

Miller, William J, Henry L Roberts, Marshall D. Shulman, *The Meaning of Communism* (Morristown, N.J.: Silver Burdett Company/Time, Inc., 1963)

Morrison, John, *Boris Yeltsin: From Bolshevik to Democrat* (New York: Dutton, 1991)

Remnick, David, *Lenin's Tomb: The Last Days of the Soviet Empire* (New York: Random House, Inc., 1993)

Richmond, Yale, *From Nyet to Da: Understanding The Russians* (Yarmouth, Maine: Intercultural Press, Inc., 1992)

Smith, Hedrick, *The New Russians* (New York: Random House, Inc.,1990)

Yeltsin, Boris, *Against the Grain* (New York: Summit Books, 1990)

Yeltsin, Boris, *Boris Yeltsin: The Struggle for Russia* (New York: Random House, Inc., 1994)

INDEX